THE POSTULANCY

THE CATHOLIC UNIVERSITY OF AMERICA
CANON LAW STUDIES
No. 386

THE POSTULANCY

A HISTORICAL CONSPECTUS AND COMMENTARY

A DISSERTATION

SUBMITTED TO THE FACULTY OF THE SCHOOL OF CANON LAW OF THE CATHOLIC UNIVERSITY OF AMERICA IN PARTIAL FULFILLMENT OF THE REQUIREMENTS FOR THE DEGREE OF DOCTOR OF CANON LAW

BY

REVEREND JAMES D. McGUIRE, O.R.S.A., J.C.L.
PRIEST OF THE PROVINCE OF ST. AUGUSTINE

THE CATHOLIC UNIVERSITY OF AMERICA PRESS
WASHINGTON, D. C.
1959

IMPRIMI POTEST:

Roman Iribarren, O.R.S.A.

Prior Provincialis

Norfolk, die 27 octobris 1958

NIHIL OBSTAT:

Romaeus W. O'Brien, O. Carm., J.C.D.

Censor Deputatus

Washingtonii, D.C., die 1 decembris 1958

IMPRIMATUR:

✠Patricius A. O'Boyle, D.D.

Archiepiscopus Washingtoniensis

Washingtonii, D.C., die 1 decembris 1958

TO MY MOTHER
AND
TO THE MEMORY OF MY FATHER

FOREWORD

The primary idea of the religious state was proclaimed by our Divine Master, Jesus Christ, in those words which were recorded for us by St. Matthew, "If thou wilt be perfect, go sell what thou hast and give to the poor; and come follow Me." [1]

From earliest times both the Church in general and the founders and lawgivers of religious orders in particular have shown concern that those who take upon themselves this life of evangelical perfection prove themselves worthy of their vocation.

The postulancy, or an initial period of probation immediately preceding the novitiate, was one of the means almost universally chosen for the attainment of this end. In the early years of monasticism the length of this probationary period was not clearly specified. It varied according to the moral worth and qualifications of the individual candidate in the judgment of his superiors. It was often quite arduous and lengthy. With St. Benedict, however, this training period was notably shortened and, while variations continued to exist, the norm set by St. Benedict became by far the most common.

In the historical presentation, since no decretal or general legislation existed on this precise point, the writer investigated the special law as contained in the various religious rules and constitutions. He has first considered those of Eastern Monasticism and then the major Rules of the West, with special emphasis of the Rule of St. Benedict, and on its widespread influence.

The particular classes of religious, the *conversi*, clerical religious, nuns, and women religious in congregations, for whom the postulancy was required, were also considered by the writer. In dealing with each class he has attempted to give importance to whatever meager papal legislation may have existed on this subject.

The second part of this study is devoted to a canonical commentary on the present discipline of the Code relative to the postulancy.

---

[1] Matt., XIX:21.

This discipline is set forth in canons 539, 540, and 541. In the treatment of these canons the chapters follow the numerical sequence that is found in the Code of Canon Law.

An attempt has been made to treat of the practical application of the norms governing the postulancy to particular cases which are either not explicitly touched upon by the common law or which are disputed among authors.

In this dissertation the practice of the Code defined in canon 490 is observed:

> Whatever is enacted for religious, although the terminology include only men, applies equally to women, unless the context or the nature of the case demands otherwise.[2]

It is hoped that this work will be useful to those who desire to know the prescriptions of the common law regarding the postulancy. It need hardly be noted, however, that in specific instances it will be necessary to consult the approved constitutions of each religious institute in order to see how the common law of the Church has been applied and adapted.

The writer wishes to express his gratitude to the Very Rev. Thomas Janices, O.R.S.A. and to the Very Rev. Roman Iribarren, O.R.S.A., former and present Prior Provincial respectively of the American Province of the Recollect Augustinian Order, for the opportunity to pursue advanced studies in Canon Law.

The writer also wishes to thank the Rev. Romaeus W. O'Brien, O. Carm., J.C.D., for his generous and scholarly guidance and the Faculty of the School of Canon Law for their helpful suggestions. Many others have contributed by counsel and encouragement to the completion of this study. To each and all of them the writer acknowledges his debt of gratitude. That the Supreme Author and sole Source of all Justice, Right and Law may provide them an acknowledgment more worthy and more lasting than a mere nominal mention in these lines is a wish which the writer commits to the hands of a generous Providence.

---

[2] "Quae de religiosis statuuntur, etsi masculino vocabulo expressa, valent etiam pari iure de mulieribus, nisi ex contextu sermonis vel ex rei natura aliud constet."

TABLE OF CONTENTS

PART II

CANONICAL COMMENTARY

THE POSTULANCY

CHAPTER I

EARLY DEVELOPMENT OF THE POSTULANCY

It can certainly be said with truth that before the time of Christ a true and proper religious state with its three essential vows of poverty, chastity, and obedience did not exist.

Although, before the deluge, in the very law of nature itself, there were to be found certain traces and foreshadowings of a religious state,[1] and, in the old written law, a religious state was prefigured in the Nazarenes and in many other groups,[2] nevertheless, a true and properly so-called religious state with the profession of the three vows was not to be found.[3]

Christ, by His example, was the first to teach the religious life *secundum se et quoad substantiam* with its three vows, and to invite all who wished to strive after perfection to embrace it.[4] The Apostles took as their rule of life the teachings and example of Christ, and in this manner of living they were soon joined by members of the early Christians who, not content with keeping only the Commandments, followed also the counsels of our Lord, especially that of poverty.[5]

From the cradle-days of the Church there were Christians who added external penances and mortifications to their internal ab-

---

[1] Cf. Genesis, IV: 26; Bellarminus, *De Membris Ecclesiae,* II, c. 5—*Opera Omnia* (8 vols., Neapoli: Pedone Lauriel, 1872), II, 220-224; Suarez, *De Auctore seu Causa Efficiente Religionis Status,* I, nn. 1-4—*Opera Omnia* (28 vols., Paris: Vivès, 1856-1878), XV, 224-225 (hereafter cited Suarez).

[2] Cf. Numbers, VI: 2 ff.; Suarez, XV, 224-225; Steiger, "De propagatione et diffusione vitae religiosae," *Periodica de Re Canonica et Morali. utilia praesertim Religiosis et Missionariis* (Brugis, 1911-19), XIII (1924), (29-33) (hereafter cited *Periodica*).

[3] Cf. Suarez, XV, 225.

[4] Matt., XIX: 11-12, 21, 29; Suarez, XV, 224-227; Steiger, *Periodica,* XIII (1924), (26).

[5] Acts, II: 44-45; IV: 32-36.

negations, in order the better to bring their bodies into subjection. Those who were devoted to these prayers, penances, privations, and other works were called *ascetae,* a word borrowed from the ancient athletes.[6] They kept themselves free from all transactions, distributed all their earthly possessions to the poor, and lived the lives of solitaries. They often took a vow of perfect chastity, or at least lived their lives in continence.[7]

As a general rule they remained in their own homes, but as far as possible they lived apart from their families. They made up a distinct class or order, midway between the clergy and the laity, and at sacred functions were preceded only by the clergy. Even after monachism was introduced, *ascetae* of this class continued in existence for some centuries.

A. EASTERN MONASTICISM

1. Development Among the Early Hermits

Because of the Decian Persecution many of the *ascetae* fled to to the deserts of Egypt. Their number was later increased by those who abandoned the cities during the persecution of the Emperor Diocletian (303). There are indications that many of them remained in the wilderness after the occasion for their life of solitude had disappeared.[8]

Others also came to the deserts, not for the purpose of escaping any persecution, but in order that they might serve God more freely, with less distraction. These were the founders of the eremetical life. The first leader of this new class of *ascetae* was St. Paul (ca. 234-347), justly called the "First Hermit."[9]

---

[6] Steiger, *Periodica,* XIII (1924), (57).

[7] Justin, *Apologia,* I, c. 15, 29—Migne, *Patrologiae Cursus Completus, Series Graeca* (161 vols., Parisiis, 1857-1866), VI, 350-375 (hereafter cited *MPG*).

[8] Cf. Bingham, *The Antiquities of the Christian Church,* Book VII, c. 1, sec. 4; Wernz, *Ius Decretalium* (6 vols. in 10, Romae-Prati, 1898-1914), III, 2, 268 (hereafter cited Wernz).

[9] Wernz, III, 2, 268; Steiger, *Periodica,* XIII (1924), (44); Heimbucher, *Die Orden und Kongregationen der katholischen Kirche* (3.ed., 2 vols., Paderborn: Schöningh, 1933-1934), I, 31 (hereafter cited Heimbucher).

The first man, however, to organize the hermits living in Upper Egypt and to guide them in the monastic life was St. Anthony of Egypt. Anthony was born in Comon, in the northern part of Egypt, about the year 251. His parents died when he was between eighteen and twenty years old, at which time he began to lead the life of a hermit. At the age of thirty-five he withdrew to the seclusion of the desert. He died on January 17, 356.[10]

Perhaps no one was more instrumental in the early development of the religious life than St. Anthony. So great was the renown of his virtue that many sought out his company in order to become his disciples. His followers, in their desire to imitate Anthony's perfection, settled near the Saint, living in caves or huts in the immediate vicinity of his hermitage at Pispir. It was from this group of followers who had gathered about him that Anthony, about 305, formed his first community.[11]

The monachism of St. Anthony was eremitical in character, and a spirit of individualism was its dominant principle.[12] Within the lifetime of its founder Christian Monachism become one of the outstanding features of the Catholic Church. One can judge how rapid must have been the spread of monachism from the fact that, by the time of Anthony's death, there were at Nitria alone five thousand monks.[13]

The Antonian monks lived in the same place, but they did not practice the common life as we know it today.[14] The discipline

---

[10] Heimbucher, I, 32-34; Allies, *The Monastic Life* (London, 1896), p. 54.

[11] Heimbucher, I, 32-34; Murphy, *St. Basil and Monasticism* (Washington, D. C.: Catholic University of America, 1930), p. 9; Clark, Lausaic *History of Palladius* (London, 1918), p. 23; Neale, *A History of the Eastern Church* (London, 1847), pp. 107-110.

[12] Cuthbert Butler, *Benedictine Monachism* (London: Longmans, Green, & Co., 1919), p. 12.

[13] Heimbucher, I, 112; Rufinus, *Historia Monachorum,* cc. 2-3—Migne, *Patrologiae Cursus Completus,* Series Latina (221 vols., Parisiis, 1844-1855), XXI, 407-433 (hereafter cited *MPL*).

[14] McNeil, *Religious of Diocesan Right* (Washington, D. C.: Catholic University of America, 1923-24), p. 4; Cayré, *Manual of Patrology and History of Theology* (Tournai: Desclée and Co., 1936), p. 502.

which St. Anthony imposed upon his followers was almost completely of a spiritual and ascetic character. Saint Athanasius (295-373)[15] in his *Vita Sancti Antonii* reproduced a discourse which furnishes us with an outline of Anthony's teachings. As far as we know, St. Anthony did not compose a written Rule as such, and the one that bears his name, and which the Maronite Monks follow, was not composed until a later date.[16]

One will look in vain for any reference in the teachings of Anthony to the fact that there was a time of formal probation among the Antonian monks. Palladius (ca. 368-431), however, related that Anthony refused to admit Paul the Simple (234-347) until he had persevered for four days, standing outside the door of Anthony's cell, and the Saint continued to try him for many more weeks.[17]

It may well be that this indeterminate first probation of the Antonian hermits played a part in the future development of an organized postulancy, as seen in the Benedictine and other Rules of the West. For monasticism in Western Europe was a direct import from the Egyptian desert, and the Antonian mode of religious life was there considered the ideal.[18] Certainly this would explain why at a later date St. Benedict inserted in his Rule this "four or five days" of knocking at the door.[19]

2. Development Among the Early Cenobites

a. *Saint Pachomius*

Saint Pachomius (ca. 292-346) may be considered as the founder of the cenobitical type of monasticism,[20] and the father of monastic Rules. He wrote the first Christian monastic "Rule" in 315.[21]

---

[15] *Vita S. Antonii—MPG,* XXVI, 838-976.

[16] Boak, *A History of Rome to 565* (New York, 1923), p. 399; Steiger, *Periodica,* XIII (1924), (45).

[17] Palladius, *Historia Lausiaca,* c. 28—*MPL,* LXXIII, 1127.

[18] Butler, *Benedictine Monachism,* p. 17.

[19] Cuthbert Butler, *Sancti Benedicti Regula Monasteriorum, Editio Critico-Practica* (Friburgi Brisgoviae, 1927), c. LXV.

[20] Smith, *Christian Monasticism* (London: Innes & Co., 1892), p. 24.

[21] Steiger, *Periodica,* XIII (1924), (57); *Regula S. Pachomii—MPL,*

He established his community upon one of the islands formed by the Nile, at Tabennisi. He required his monks to live under one roof, with strict discipline and subjection to a superior. The Rule composed by Pachomius accurately determined the manner of living which was to be followed by those who placed themselves under his direction. It prescribed community life within the monastic limits, under obedience and poverty.[22] Pachomius was able to gather together in a single monastery several hundred cenobites, and other houses were soon founded and united under the authority of what we may call a Superior General. Around the year 400 there were about five thousand monks following this manner of religious life.[23]

The Forty-Ninth Chapter of the Rule of St. Pachomius sets forth the provisions regarding the period of probation for candidates who seek admission to the community:

> Si quis accesserit ad ostium monasterii, volens saeculo renuntiare, et fratrum aggregari numero, non habebit intrandi libertatem, sed prius nuntiabitur Patri monasterii, et *manebit paucis diebus foris ante januam*, et docebitur orationem Dominicam ac psalmos, quantos poterit ediscere; et diligenter sui experimentum dabit, ne forte mali quidpiam fecerit, et tubatus at horam timore discesserit, aut sub aliqua potestate sit; et utrum possit renuntiare parentibus suis, et propriam contemnere facultatem. Se enim viderint aptum ad orationem et ad omnia, tunc docebitur et reliquas monasterii disciplinas, quas servare debeat et facere, quibusque servire, sive in collecta omnium fratrum, sive in domo cui tradendus est, sive in vescendi ordine; ut instructus, atque perfectus, in omni opere bono, fratribus copuletur. Tunc nudabunt eum vestimentis saecularibus, et induent eum habitu monachorum, tradentque ostiario, ut orationis tempore adducat eum in conspectum omnium fratrum: sedebitque in loco, in quo ei praeceptum fuerit. Vestimenta autem, quae secum detulerat, accipient que huic rei propositi sunt, et inferent in reposi-

XXIII, 61-86; Palladius, *Historia Lausiaca*, c. 28—*MPL*, LXXIII, 1127; Mackean, *Christian Monasticism in Egypt* (New York: Macmillan, 1920), p. 91.

[22] *Regula S. Pachomii—MPL*, XXIII, 61-86; Vermeersch, "Religious Life," *Catholic Encyclopedia*, XII, 750.

[23] Cayré, *Manual of Patrology and History of Theology*, p. 504.

> torium, et erunt in potestate principis monasterii.[24] (Writer's Italics)

Among the precepts of St. Pachomius we find:

> Si quis ad monasterium accesserit volens fieri novitius, precationem ei evangelicam porrigent, et psalmos docebunt. *Maneat porro ad monasterii fores,* ibique probetur; quidquid autem alii norunt fratres, istic et ipse addiscat. Quo facto, saecularibus eum vestibus exuent, et novitiorum habitu vestient.[25] (Writer's Italics)

From these two passages it seems that St. Pachomius required two distinct periods of probation, which correspond more or less to the postulancy and the novitiate now demanded by the Code of Canon Law. During the initial period of probation, or the postulancy, the aspirant to the religious life was to be subjected to an examination in order to determine whether his desire to embrace the cenobitic life was sincere or not. Until this examination was completed with satisfaction, it seems that the candidate was not to be received within the monastery proper, but was to be provided for outside the gates. The Rule is silent as to what the exact duration of the postulancy should be, merely requiring that the one seeking admission should remain outside the monastery door for a few days. Cassian (ca. 360-430/5), however, was of the opinion that this period lasted for ten days.[26]

Although the postulancy was not yet formally constituted, nor the duration of this probationary period, nor the discipline nor the obligations of the postulants expressly determined, yet there was by the time St. Pachomius (ca. 292-346) a certain probation and preparation already prescribed by Rule. It seems, therefore, that we can conclude that certain vestiges of the postulancy were already in existence by the time of the Rule of St. Pachomius.

---

[24] *Regula Pachomii,* c. 49—*MPL,* XXIII, 70.

[25] *Precepta Pachomii,* c. 15—*MPG,* XL, 950.

[26] *De Institutis Coenobiorum; Collationes XXIV,* Lib. IV, c. 3—*Corpus Scriptorum Ecclesiasticorum Latinorum (CSEL)* (Editum consilio et impensis Academiae Litterarum Caesareae Vindobonensis, Vindobonae: apud Geroldi Filium, 1866—), Vol. XVII, Pars I, 49-50.

b. *Schenute*

Schenute was born at Schenalolet, in the district of Akhim. The exact year of his birth is unknown, but it took place somewhere between the years 332 and 350. In 371, he became a monk at the large double monastery of Deir-el-Abiad (White Monastery, so called because its external wall was constructed of white stones). This monastery was under the rule of his uncle Bgol, whom he succeeded as abbot in 388. He continued to hold this position until the time of his death, which occurred about the year 451 or 452.[27]

The Rule of St. Pachomius formed the basis of government for the monks under Schenute.[28] This Rule, however, was subject to various modifications and was made more severe under Bgol and Schenute, the latter of whom was the most influential monastic head and perhaps the most powerful man in Egypt during his time. At his death it is estimated that he had in his charge 2,200 monks and 1,800 nuus.[29]

In monasteries subject to Schenute's jurisdiction no candidate was to be admitted, unless he had beforehand undergone a preliminary probation in the guest-house for one month or even longer. At the close of this period he was to be examined in regard to his former way of life and the motives impelling him to seek entrance into religion.[30]

In both the monasteries and nunneries over which Schenute ruled there were established schools for boys and girls respectively. It is not clear, however, whether these schools were instituted for the purpose of training future candidates for the monastic life, after the fashion of our modern day Apostolic Colleges or Minor Seminaries, or whether the alumni of these schools were also required, if they desired to embrace this form of the religious life, to undergo the initial period of probation before the door of the

---

27 Ott, "Schenute," *Catholic Encyclopedia*, XIII, 527.

28 Ladeuze, *Étude sur le Cénobitisme Pakhomien* (Louvain, 1898), p. 206; Mackean, *Christian Monasticism in Egypt*, p. 112.

29 Leipoldt, *Schenute von Atripe, Texte und Untersuchungen zur altchristlichen Literatur*, N. F., Bd. X, Hft. I (Leipzig, 1903), p. 93.

30 Leipoldt, *Schenute von Atripe*, pp. 112-113.

monastery and in the guest-house, before they could be granted admission to the monastery proper.[31] Whatever may be the case, in the norms set down by Schenute we have a clearer vestige of the postulancy than was to be found in the Rule of St. Pachomius. The outstanding mark of this initial period of probation as set forth by the Rule of St. Pachomius and in the version modified by Schenute seems to be its indeterminate character with regard to the length of the time of probation. This elasticity seems to have left its mark upon many subsequent Rules which were influenced by the Rule of St. Basil, which in turn was patterned upon that of St. Pachomius.

3. Development in the Rule of Saint Basil

Saint Basil, called the "Father of Eastern Monasticism," [32] was born in Cappadocia, about the year 329 or 330. After spending his early life in the pursuits of learning, he resolved to enter the monastic life. He made an intimate study of the various types of monasticism obtaining in Egypt, Palestine, Coele Syria, and Mesopotamia. Returning to Pontus near Neocaesarea about 358, he organized a community of ascetics on the banks of the Iris. In the year 370 he was appointed Bishop of Caesarea in Cappadocia, and he died there on January 1, 379.[33]

Saint Basil left two monastic Rules to direct his followers along the paths of virtue. These are known as the *Regulae Fusius Tractatae* and the *Regulae Brevius Tractatae*.[34]

The first of these was not a monastic rule in the ordinary sense of the word, but rather a synopsis of fifty-five lectures, in which the Saint treated the main points of the religious life according to the Scriptures. The Shorter Rule was nothing more than a number of answers of the master to questions put to him by his disciples.

---

[31] Ladeuze, *Étude sur le Cénobitisme Pakhomien*, p. 313.

[32] Heimbucher, I, 121; *Vitae Patrum—MPL*, LXXIII, 294.

[33] Clark, *St. Basil the Great* (Cambridge, 1913), p. 26.

[34] *Regulae Sancti Basilii—MPG*, XXXI, 890-1051.

Rufinus (345-410) made a Latin translation of these Rules, which was adopted by some of the monasteries of the West.[35]

The conditions for admission into the monasteries subject to the jurisdiction of St. Basil are contained in the Tenth *Interrogatio* of the Longer Rule. Basil tells us very little about the actual regulations for entrance into the monasteries of Cappadocia. He states that aspirants to the religious life are to be gladly welcomed. "Since our Saviour Jesus Christ has said, 'Come unto Me, all you that labor and are heavy burdened, and I will give you rest,' (Matt., XI: 28), it is dangerous to reject those who desire by means of us to draw near unto the Lord, and to take upon themselves His easy yoke and the burden of His commandments which raises us to heaven." [36]

Yet, the candidate was to submit to an examination regarding his past life, his character and his ability to bear the burdens of the religious life. Even those whose past life had not been wholly exemplary, or whose morals were not above all question, were not immediately to be dismissed, but were rather to be subjected to suitable spiritual exercises, so that the superior might be able to decide whether their entrance into the monastery could be safely permitted. If a man who had acquired some distinction in the world desired admittance to the company of the monks, he was to be given the most menial tasks to perform, in order that his humility might be put to the test. Only when he had successfully passed all the tests, applied by those who were experts in these matters, was he to be included "in the number of those who have dedicated themselves to the Lord." [37]

It seems that St. Basil left much much concerning the admission of candidates to the discretion of the superior. The determining factor in the admission into the Basilian monasteries appears to have been the superior's judgment about the qualifications of the candidate. Although nothing definite on the length of the proba-

---

[35] *Regulae Sancti Basilii Episcopi Cappadociae ad Monachos—MPL,* CIII, 483-554.

[36] *Reg. Fus. Tract.,* 10—*MPG,* XXXI, 943.

[37] *Reg. Fus. Tract.,* 10—*MPG,* XXXI, 943; Morison, *St. Basil and His Rule* (London, 1912), p. 87.

tionary period can be accurately deduced from a reading of his Rule, it seems safe to conclude with Bakalarcyzk[38] that the preparation, probation and emendation of life insisted on by St. Basil were impossible within a short period of time. It also appears probable that the initial examination of the candidate, which was so thorough as to require his close observation and hence his residence in or near the monastery, might well be considered as a fore-runner, if a primitive one, of the modern institute of the postulancy.

4. Development in Other Rules

There is another Oriental Rule of antiquity which is handed down as having been composed by a number of abbots who were meeting together to discuss questions of mutual interest. Hence this Rule is not proper to any one man and is known as the Rule of Saints Serapion, Macarius, Paphnutius and the other Macarius.[39]

The seventh Chapter of this Rule contains the regulations for the admission of new candidates to the monastery:

> Quidquid acciderit, aut justum quid fuerit, memores esse debetis: 'In tribulatione patientes; in operibus honesti. Nolite vos invicem ad iracundiam provocare, sed semper bona sectamini.' (Rom., XII; Eph., VI). Ii, qui tales sunt, cum de saeculi hujus illecebris liberari voluerint, appropiantes monasterio, *hebdomada pro foribus jaceant*: nulli cum eis de fratribus jungantur, et semper dura et laboriosa eis proponantur. Si vero perseveraverint pulsantes, eis non negetur ingressus; sed is qui praeest, Pater hujusmodi homines introire permittat, et qualiter vitam fratrum, vel Regulam tenere possint, ostendat.[40] (Writer's Italics).

From the prescriptions of this Rule one can readily see that it was the general consensus among the abbots of the different

---

[38] Bakalarcyzk, *De Novitiatu*, The Catholic University of America, Canon Law Studies, n. 36 (Washington, D. C.: The Catholic University of America, 1927), p. 19.

[39] *Codex Regularum S. Benedicti Abbatis Anianensis—MPL,* CIII, 435-436.

[40] *Regula Sanctorum Serapionis, Macarii, Paphnutii et alterius Macarii,* c. 7—*MPL,* CIII, 437-438.

monasteries that the aspirant to the religious life was not to be granted easy and ready entrance into the monastery. He was for a week to stand outside the doors of the monastery, begging admission from the monks with whom he might come in contact, and they, far from granting his request, were to treat him rather harshly. It was only after he had successfully undergone this first trial that the candidate was to be allowed to enter the monastery. If we may draw anything from the words of this Rule, it seems that even this eventual permission was a rather grudging one, "eis non negetur ingressus." This Rule would lead one to believe, then, that a period of initial probation, or a postulancy, is an institute that is as old as the organized forms of the religious life itself, and one whose necessity and utility have always been recognized.

Before passing on to the Rules of the West, one should point out that the women religious of this period who belonged to monastic establishments, especially those that were patterned after the Pachomian model, followed the same Rule, *mutatis mutandis,* as the monks. Hence there are no changes of importance in regard to the initial probationary period in these communities of women.[41]

B. WESTERN MONASTICISM

1. Rules Before Saint Benedict

a. *Rule of Saint Augustine*

Saint Augustine was born at Tagaste, Africa, in the year 354. Because of a custom then prevalent in that country he did not receive baptism as an infant, and it was not until he was thirty-three years of age that he was baptized by St. Ambrose in Milan. Following his conversion, Augustine returned to his native land and there in Tagaste, together with several of his companions, began to lead a monastic life. It was from this community that he was taken to be invested with the sacerdotal dignity in the Church of Hippo, of which he afterwards became bishop. There he founded another monastery in 391. As bishop of Hippo, Augustine intro-

[41] *Vita Pachomii,* n. 22—*MPL,* LXXIII, 227-282.

duced in 396 the common manner of life among the secular clergy.[42]

The monasteries of monks certainly differed from those of the clerics. We may believe that St. Augustine did not have it in mind to institute two religious orders. Because, however, of the diversity of the life that was led in each, he had laid the foundations, from which later came the Order of Hermits of St. Augustine and the Order of Clerics Regular of St. Augustine.[43]

The Rule of St. Augustine was most probably adopted for men from his Letter 211, which he wrote to his sister and her community. There is absolutely no evidence as to the identity of the adaptor. Simple conjecture seems to point to Augustine himself, for the authenticity of Letter 211 to the nuns is beyond question; his Rule *ad Servos Dei* is in evident and certain concord with this letter; the time of the adaptation, according to present research, must be placed in the fifth century, that is, within the lifetime of St. Augustine.[44]

In the Rule of St. Augustine itself there are no provisions regarding a period of probation or the training of candidates. Nevertheless, it is unthinkable that an able legislator like St. Augustine did not have some definite provisions for the reception of candidates into his monasteries. Perhaps each monastery had a set of auxiliary laws, similar to the constitutions of our present religious orders, in which such directives were contained; or possibly it was left to the discretion of the one in charge of the individual monastery to try aspirants and admit candidates to the monastic life as he deemed fitting in each particular case. Thus Augustine, for whom obedience and the position of authority of the superior were of the greatest importance, may have considered that this point of a probationary period was implicitly taken care of by his strong insistence on the complete obedience due the superior.[45]

---

[42] Currier, *History of Religious Orders* (New York: Murphy & McCarthy, 1899), p. 305; Fernandez, *De Figura Juridica Ordinis Recollectorum S. Augustini* (Romae: apud Aedes Universitatis Gregorianae, 1938), p. 17.

[43] Fernandez, *loc. cit.*

[44] Fernandez, *ibid.*, p. 55.

[45] *Regula S. Augustini ad Servos Dei*, c. 11—*MPL*, XXXII, 1381.

b. *Rule of John Cassian*

John Cassian was born probably in Provence about the year 360. The son of wealthy parents, he received a good education and as a youth visited the Holy Land. While in Bethlehem, Cassian assumed the obligations of the monastic life, and his desire for greater perfection drove him from there to the deserts of Egypt. He visited the solitaries most famous for their holiness. While in Rome as a delegate of St. John Chrysostom he was ordained a priest. About 415 he was in Marseilles, where he founded two monasteries, one for men, over the tomb of St. Victor, and the other for women. His personal influence and his writings contributed greatly to the diffusion of monasticism in the West. His two great works are the *Institutes*, which is mainly taken up with what belongs to the outer man and the customs of the *coenobia*; and the *Conferences*, which deals with the training of the inner man and the perfection of the heart. Cassian is credited with being the first to introduce the Rules of Eastern Monasticism into the West. He died probably near Marseilles about the year 435.[46]

Both of his famous works were written for the guidance of the first abobts of Lerins, as well as for Cassian's own monastery at Marseilles.

In the Fourth Book of Cassian's *Institutes* two of the chapters, the third and the seventh, deal with the admission of candidates into the religious life.[47]

Chapter Three treats of the ordeal by which one who is to be received in the monastery is tested, and contains the following regulations:

> One, then, who seeks to be admitted to the discipline of the monastery is never received before he gives, *by lying outside the doors for ten days or even longer*, an evidence of his perseverance and desire, as well as of humility and patience. And when, prostrate at the feet of all the brethren

[46] Cf. Chapman, *John Cassian* (Cambridge: Cambridge University Press, 1959).

[47] *De Institutis Coenobiorum,* lib. IV, nn. 3, 7—*CSEL,* Vol. XVII, Pars I, pp. 49-50.

> that pass by, and of set purpose repelled and scorned by all of them, as if he was wanting to enter the monastery not for the sake of religion but because he was obliged; and when, too, covered with many insults and affronts, he has given a practical proof of his steadfastness, and has shown what he will be like in temptations by the way he has borne the disgrace; and when, with the ardour of his soul thus ascertained, he is admitted, then they enquire with the utmost care whether he is contaminated by a single coin from his former possessions clinging to him. . . . (Writer's Italics).

Chapter Seven contains the following directives:

> When, then, anyone has been received and proved by that persistence of which we have spoken, and, laying aside his own garments, has been clad in those of the monastery, he is not allowed to mix at once with the congregation of the brethren, but is given into the charge of an Elder, who lodges apart not far from the entrance of the monastery, and is entrusted with the care of strangers and guests, and bestows all his diligence in receiving them kindly. And when he has served there *for a whole year* without any complaint, and has given evidence of service towards strangers, being thus initiated in the first rudiments of humility and patience, and by long practice in it acknowledged, when he is to be admitted from this into the congregation of the brethren he is handed over to another Elder, who is placed over ten of the juniors, who are entrusted to him by the abbot, and whom he both teaches and governs in accord with the arrangement which we read of in Exodus as made by Moses. (Exod., XVIII: 25).[48] (Writer's Italics).

From these excerpts it is evident that the Deltan Monks required at least a year and ten days to be spent in the postulancy, and Cassian, who had lived with them for a time and who was one of their most ardent admirers, set down the same requirements for those who came to his monasteries seeking entrance. This period of trial was divided into two parts; the first was very short, but was to be at least ten days, and this period was to be

[48] *De Institutis Coenobiorum,* Lib. IV, nn. 3, 7. Translation from Nicene and Post-Nicene Fathers, Second Series, XI (New York: Christian Literature Co., 1894), pp. 219-221.

spent outside the monastery; the second part of the Cassian postulancy was to last for one year, during which time the postulant was obliged to live in the guest-house, serving as a menial and waiting upon the visitors to the monastery. It must, however, always be remembered that these directives were quite elastic, and much was left to the judgment and prudence of the superior, who felt free to lengthen or shorten the time of trial according to the circumstances of the particular case. The requirements which were drawn up by Cassian in his *Institutes* take on added importance when we recall the great effect that this work had upon St. Benedict and subsequent founders of religious orders.[49]

c. *Rule of Saint Caesarius of Arles*

Saint Caesarius was born at Chalon-sur-Saône in Burgundy in 470 or 471 and entered the monastery of Lerins when he was quite young. Because he became sick the abbot sent him to Arles to recuperate, and there he was ordained. In 502 he was chosen Bishop of Arles, which see he ruled for forty years until his death in 542. Caesarius was the author of two Rules, one for men and the other for women. The Rule for monks is based on that of the monastery of Lerins, as handed down by oral tradition. This Rule soon gave way to the Rule of St. Columbanus, and with the latter eventually to that of St. Benedict. The Rule for nuns, however, had a different fate. It was the work of his whole lifetime, and into it he poured all his prudence, tenderness, experience and foresight. It borrows heavily from St. Augustine and John Cassian. This Rule was first put into effect by his sister, St. Caesaria, who was the abbess of the monastery for nuns (at Aliscamps, outside the walls of Arles) which counted two-hundred members at the death of its founder.[50]

In the third Chapter of the Rule for nuns we read:

> Ei ergo quae Deo inspirante convertitur non licebit statim habitum religionis assumere, nisi antea in multis experimentis

---

[49] Martène, *In Regula S. P. Benedicti Commentata,* c. 73—*MPL,* LXVI, 930; *ibid.,* c. 42—*MPL,* LXVI, 670.

[50] Malnory, *St. Cesaire, Evêque d'Arles* (Paris, 1894), p. 257; "Caesarius of Arles," *Catholic Encyclopedia,* III, 135.

> fuerit voluntas illius approbata; sed uni ex senioribus tradita annum integrum in eo quo venit habitu perseveret. De ipso tamen habito mutando, vel lecto in schola habendo, sit in potestate prioris; et quomodo personam vel compunctionem viderit, ita vel celerius, vel tardius studeat temperare.[51]

After Caesarius wrote this Rule, he later amended and corrected it in what is known as a *Recapitulatio*. In Chapter Eight of this *Recapitulatio* there is the following:

> Quaecumque ad conversionem venerit, in salutatorio ei frequentius Regula relegatur; et si prompta et libera voluntate professa fuerit se omnia Regulae instituta complecturam, tandiu ibi sit quandiu Abbatissae justum ac rationabile visum fuerit; si vero Regulam dixerit se non posse complere, penitus non excipiatur.[52]

In the Rule for monks the length of the probationary period is not determined. The candidate, however, had to go through a period of training before he could be considered eligible to receive the religious habit.

From the two passages quoted above from the Rule for nuns we see that at first the Saint set down that immediate entrance to the convent was not to be granted. No one was to be admitted until she had previously been tried under one of the senior sisters for the period of one year. This period, however, was merely a norm, and the superioress, at her discretion, could grant an earlier admission or retard the admission of the aspirants according as she judged wisest in each case.

In the *Recapitulatio* St. Caesarius seemed to do away with the normative period of one year altogether, and to leave the entire matter to the judgment of the superioress. Another requirement which was not in his Rule proper was set down here, namely that the period of probation was to be spent in the parlor, where the Rule was to be read to the candidate frequently. It seems a safe conclusion, then, that St. Caesarius demanded a period of probation and trial comparable to the postulancy, but this was indefinite,

---

[51] *Regula Caesarii ad Virgines,* c. 3—*MPL,* LXVII, 1107.

[52] *Recapitulatio—MPL,* LXVII, 1118.

and much concrening it was left to prudent judgment of the superioress.

This Rule has been thought worthy of special mention because it had a marked effect on the Rule of St. Benedict. The probationary details which are contained here are seen again in a modified form in the Benedictine Rule.[53]

2. Development in the Rule of Saint Benedict

Saint Benedict was born at Nursia, Italy, in the year 480, and at the age of seventeen renounced the world and the wealth and position of his parents by taking refuge in a cave at Subiaco in the Sabine Mountains. There he led the life of a hermit for several years, during which time he established twelve monasteries for his disciples over which he ruled as Abbot. Forced by persecution to leave Subiaco, he settled at Monte Cassino in 529, where he founded a large monastery and composed his famous Rule. His sister, St. Scholastica, established herself in a monastery near this mountain, and Benedict directed her in her religious life, as he did many nuns in the neighborhood. He died forty days after the death of his sister in 553.[54]

It is the fifty-eighth Chapter of his Rule which contains the provisions for the admission of candidates into the monastic life.[55]

This Chapter, *"De Disciplina Suscipiendorum Fratrum,"* prescribed:

> Noviter veniens quis ad conversionem, non ei facilis tribuatur ingressus; sec sicut ait Apostolus: 'Probate Spiritus, si ex Deo sunt.' (Joan., I: 4). Ergo si veniens perseveraverit pulsans, et illatas sibi injurias et difficultatem ingressus, *post quatuor aut quinque dies* visus fuerit patienter portare, et persistere petitioni suae: annuatar ei ingressus, et sit in cella hospitum *paucis diebus*. Postea autem sit in cella novitiorum. . . .[56] (Writer's Italics).

[53] Chapman, *St. Benedict and the Sixth Century* (London: Sheed & Ward, 1929), pp. 76-81.

[54] Montalambert, *The Monks of the West* (New York: Longmans, Greene and Co., 1896), pp. 305-327.

[55] Cuthbert Butler, *Sancti Benedicti Regula Monasteriorum*, c. LVIII.

[56] Butler, *loc. cit.; MPL*, LXVI, 803.

Hence we see that St. Benedict, like so many of the other monastic legislators, was not in favor of a too ready admission to the monastery. The discipline of his Rule also required that all who wished to enter the monastery be refused permission to enter until after four or five days of patient knocking at the door. Even when the candidate's patience was rewarded and he was finally allowed to enter, it was not to the monastery proper that he was admitted, but to the guest-house, where he was to spend several days waiting upon the guests and visitors of the monastery. Only after these two short probationary periods was the aspirant permitted access to the novitiate. St. Benedict retained "the four or five days of knocking" that were demanded by some of the ancient Deltan monks, but he shortened the year which they required to be spent in the guest-house to a few days. The actual term "postulancy" was not used by St. Benedict in his Rule, but it is quite certain that while the word is not found there, at least some form of this institute as we know it is in evidence.

Of course, there is no indication in this Rule, nor in any of the earlier ones, that this time of probation was required under pain of invalidity of the candidate's subsequent profession of vows. In all of these Rules, it was understood that the superior could shorten this period at his own discretion, even if no express mention was made of this fact.

The majority of Benedictine offshoots followed the example of St. Benedict, and required only a few days to be devoted to this preliminary period.

3. Development in Rules After Saint Benedict

a. *Rule of Saint Isidore of Seville*

Born at Cartagena, Spain, about 560, Saint Isidore received his elementary education at the Cathedral School of Seville. It is not known with certainty whether he himself became a monk, but he had a high esteem for all religious orders. In 599 he succeeded his brother Leander in the Metropolitan See of Seville, and immediately constituted himself the protector of the monks. His *Regula Monachorum*, which he probably wrote before he was elevated to the episcopacy, is a manner of life prescribed for monks, and also in a general way deals with the monastic state. St. Isidore died on April 4, 636.[57]

The fourth Chapter of his Rule, which is entitled *"De Conversis,"* stated:

> Qui vero renuncians saeculo ad monasterium venerit, non statim in coetum delegandus est monachorum. Vitam enim uniuscujusque in hospitalis servitio *tribus mensibus* considerari opportet, quibus peractis ad coetum sanctae congregationis accedere. Neque enim intus suscipi quemquam convenit, nisi *prius foris positus,* ejus humilitas, sive patientia comprobetur.[58] (Writer's Italics).

Basically the requirements of Isidore's Rule were the same as those of the earlier monastic lawgivers, i.e., a not too ready admission, and then some time spent, not strictly within the monastery itself, but in its guest-house, by serving as a menial. In this instance the time of the period of probation was three months, which was a much more stringent requirement than the few days demanded by St. Benedict, and yet far less demanding than the one year of the Deltan monks.

b. *Rule of Saint Fructuosus*

After the death of his parents St. Fructuosus retired as a hermit to a desert in Galicia, where he later started his monastery of Complutum. For a time he acted as the Abbot of this foundation, and then again sought the solitude of the desert. During his lifetime he founded nine monasteries and a convent for virgins. In 654 he became the Bishop of Dumium and in 656 Archbishop of Braga, in Portugal. He was the author of two Rules. The first (twenty-five chapters) was destined for the monastery of Complutum, and the second, called the "Common Rule" (twenty chapters) referred to a union of monasteries governed by an abbot-

---

57 Cf. Quiles, *San Isidoro de Sevilla* (Espasa-Calpe Argentina, S. A., 1945).

58 *Concordia Regularum Patrum—MPL,* CIII, 1275-76.

bishop and was addressed chiefly to the superiors of monasteries.[59]

It is the twenty-first Chapter of his *Regula Monachorum, "De Converso, qualiter debeat suscipi,"* which ordained:

> Conversum de saeculo Patrum decreta docent non suscipiendum in monasterio, nisi experimentum sui opere et penuriam opprobriis dederit et conviciis: *quique decem diebus persistens ad januam coenobii* orationibus et jejuniis, patientiae et humilitati operam dederit. Sicque *anno integro* uni spiritali traditus seniori non statim comiscendus erit congregationi, neque interna fratum diversoria accedet, sed delegata in exteriore corte cellula perfruetur, ubi omnem sinceriter exerceat obedientiam: hopitibus sive peregrinis stramina comportabit, aquam califaciens pedibus, et omnia humiliter ministeria execebit, fascemque lignorum suo quotidie dorso ferens hebdomadariis tribuet. Atque ita in omni penuria et vilitate subactus, expleto anno, probatus moribus et laboribus elimatus, percepta in ecclesia benedictione, fratum societate donetur: unique decano delegetur cunctis bonorum operum exercitiis edocendus. Quod si quilibet conversus, bonis ac puris moribus enitens, abbatis vel aliorum fratum spiritalium fuerit judicio comprobatus, pro merito et puritate suae conscientiae celerius poterit fratrum consortiis misceri secundum quod abbatis vel fratrum ob timorem consuerit deliberatio faciendum.[60] (Writer's Italics).

This rule contained the same rather strict requirements for admission to the monastery as did the Rules which governed the Deltan monks of Egypt. Ten days were spent in the asking of permission to enter and in the patient acceptance of all rebuffs. When finally the monk-to-be obtained admission to the monastery, he was ordered to pass a whole year in the service of the guests and visitors of the monastery, during which time he was under the charge of one of the senior monks. Only after he had successfully undergone this period of scrutiny and probation was he permitted to associate with the other monks as a novice. Here again we see

---

[59] Cf. Nock, *Vita Sancti Fructuosi of St. Valerius, Abbot of San Pedro de Montes with a Translation, Introduction and Commentary,* Studies in Medieval History, New Series, Vol. VII (Washington, D. C.: Catholic University of America Press, 1946).

[60] *Concordia Regularum Patrum—MPL,* CIII, 1277-78.

that there was a time of initial testing of the candidates for the religious life, which served the same purpose as our modern postulancy, although it was not at that time referred to as such.

c. *The Tarnation Rule and the "Regula Magistri"*

The Tarnation Rule probably takes its name from the monastery at Tarnat in Vienne, France, which was founded in 516, but the Rule appears to have been written for the monastery of St. Maurice in Switzerland (470), now an abbacy *nullius*. In its opening chapter it contained the following regulations for the admission of aspirants to the monastic life:

> Si quis fidei ardore succensus renuntians saeculo monasterium magnae dispositionis elegerit expetendum, non confestim licentia tribuatur intrandi, sed primum studiosius indagetur utrum voluntarie, an necessitate aliqua coactus advenerit, aut si nulla servitutis conditione obnoxius teneatur. Quod cum ad abbatis notitiam praeposito nuniante pervenerit, *uni de senioribus deputatus tandiu jubeatur advenientibus deservire*, quousque devotio ejus fuerit patientia teste monstrata . . .[61] (Writer's Italics).

The author of the *Regula Magistri* is not known with certainty, but this Rule is often attributed to the Deacon Vigilantius. We do know that this Rule was composed in Gaul, and that it drew heavily upon that of St. Benedict. It was the eighty-eighth Chapter that treated of the requisites for entrance into the monastery, in the form namely of a question to which the Master responded:

> Cum de omnibus supra dictis conventus novus frater Regulae per abbatem de stabilitate firmanda, aut per rerum suarum eleemosynam, aut per donationem monasterio, aut per chartam fidejussoris poenalem, aut si ignotus per juramenti fidem, duorum tamen mensium spatium in inducias ad tractandum accipat. Laborando tamen cum fratribus contentus annonae communi mensura, vel regulae disciplina et excommunicationum, ut et mores monasterii probet, et a monasterio ipse probetur; et secum tractet, si debeat se ad Deum firmare, aut ad diabolum expeditius remeare. In quibus duobus mensibus sub cura illorum fratrum, qui peregrinos custodiunt, et ipsi simi-

[61] *Concordia Regularum Patrum—MPL*, CIII, 1284.

> liter ex improviso custodiatur, et in cella peregrinorum dormiat, ut ingressus illius, vel exitus in monasterio custodum praesentia videatur. Et omni hora si alicubi a conventu fratrum secesserit sollicite a custodibus requiratur, ne forte anticipet ambulare sine vale cum furto.[62]

Both of the above quoted Rules agreed in denying to the would-be religious too easy an admission. Both prescribed that once he is admitted he shall spend some time under one of the older monks, not within the monastery itself, but in that section which offers accommodations to the guests and visitors of the monastery. The major difference between these two Rules on this point of a postulancy was the time required by each. The first appears to set down one year as a dispensable norm to be followed, while the second demands but a two months' service in the guest-house. But both of these Rules contained an unmistakable, if primitive, vestige of the present institute of the postulancy.

C. THE DIFFUSION OF THE BENEDICTINE RULE

There is in Mansi a reference of at least doubtful authenticity which relates that the II Council of Rome (595 A.D.), under Pope Gregory I, gave approval and confirmation to the Rule of St. Benedict.[63]

It was during the sixth and seventh centuries that the great monastic foundations of Ireland were sending into Europe a steady stream of missionaries. Perhaps no other establishment could match the Irish monasteries in Italy, Gaul, Germany and Switzerland for their learning and holiness. The Rule that most of the Irish monks followed was that of St. Columban (543-615), but it proved so strict that it was gradually replaced by the milder one of St. Benedict. The Roman spirit little by little supplanted the Celtic, so that within two centuries the Benedictine Rule was in quite general use in Western Europe.

---

[62] *Concordia Regularum Patrum—MPL,* CIII, 1292.

[63] Nota Severini Binii in Mansi, *Sacrorum Conciliorum Nova et Amplissima Collectio* (53 vols. in 60, Paris, Leipzig, Arnhem, 1901-1927), X, 477 (hereafter cited Mansi).

Some of the local councils of the time also contained canons which encouraged the monasteries under their jurisdiction to take up the Rule of St. Benedict. The Council of Autun, held in 670, declared that "it is proper that Abbots and monks teach and follow the Rule of St. Benedict." [64]

A Council presided over by St. Boniface at either Ratisbon or Augsburg, Germany, in 743, stated that "monks and nuns should endeavor to direct and govern their monasteries according to the Rule of the Holy Father Benedict." [65]

Both the Council of Mainz[66] and the II Council of Rheims[67] in 813 urged their monasteries to follow the Benedictine Rule. The II Council of Chalon-sur-Saône, held in the same year, made the observation that "almost all the monasteries in this locality follow the Rule of St. Benedict." [68]

The Benedictine Rule, then, gradually replaced more and more the various earlier Rules. While in various Benedictine off-shoots there might be found some modifications on some point or other, or adaptations to suit some particular need or circumstance, it seems safe to conclude that by the eleventh century it was practically a universal custom in the Western Church for all the candidates for the religious life to undergo some form of initial probation comparable to our postulancy, and became of the influence of St. Benedict's Rule its duration as a period of probation was generally rather short and even completely dispensable within the judgment of the superior.

---

[64] Can. 15—Mansi, XI, 124; *Monumenta Germaniae Historia, Legum Sectio, III, Concilia, I, Concilia Aevi Merovingici* (ed. F. Maassen, Hannoverae, 1893), 221 (the *Monumenta* will be hereafter cited *MGH*).

[65] Can. 7—Mansi, XII, 367; *MGH, Legum Sectio III, Concilia, II, Concilia Aevi Karolini, Pars I* (recensuit Albertus Werminghoff, Hannoverae et Lipsiae, 1906), 4.

[66] Can. 11—Mansi, XIV, 68; *MGH, Legum Sectio III, Concilia, II, Concilia Aevi Karolini, Pars I*, 263.

[67] Can. 9—Mansi, XIV, 78; *MGH, Legum Sectio III, ibid.*, 255.

[68] Can. 22—Mansi, XIV, 98; *MGH, Legum Sectio III, ibid.*, 278.

CHAPTER II

LATER DEVELOPMENT OF A POSTULANCY

A. Postulancy for "Conversi"

1. *Early Development of "Conversi"*

Since the *conversi* in institutes of men religious with perpetual vows constitute one of the classes for whom the postulancy is now required by the common law,[1] one should here recount something of the history of this *"conversi"* institute with especial reference to the necessity of a postulancy.

Until the eleventh century in the history of religious orders there was no clear-cut and legally established class distinction. The main reason for this was probably the fact that the monastic state had no clerical connotation, and when a priest entered a monastery his ordination made him no more a monk than were his lay companions in religion. In fact, the majority of St. Benedict's monks were not clerics, and all performed manual labor. The word *"conversi"* was originally used to designate those who, in adult life, voluntarily renounced the world and entered a religious order to do penance and to lead a life of greater perfection. The renouncing of the world was known as the *conversio a saeculo*, which had as its object a reform or change of life, the *conversio morum*, and hence the term *conversi* or the "converted." The *conversi* were thus distinguished from the *oblati* and *nutriti* or those who, as children, were presented or offered (*oblati*) by their parents to the religious life.[2]

The introduction, then, of *conversi* as a new class of religious,

[1] Can. 539, § 1.

[2] Haring, *Grundzüge des katholischen Kirchenrechts* (3. ed., 2 vols., Graz, 1924), Vol. II, p. 759; Mratène-Durand, *Thesaurus Novus Ancedotorum* (5 vols., Lutetiae Parisiorum, 1717), IV, 1547-1652 (hereafter cited *Thesaurus*).

who were especially destined for manual labor among reformed branches in the Benedictine Order in the eleventh century, was an historical innovation in monasticism.[3]

It is to St. Ulrich of Zell (1029-1093) and Blessed William of Hirsau (d. 1091), two zealous promoters of the Benedictine reform, that the credit must be given for the rudimentary foundation of the *conversi* institute as we know it today. Blessed William, after his election as Abbot of Hirsau, composed a famous work of monastic usage, *Consuetudines Hirsaugienses,* in which he set down abundant provisions and regulations for the *conversi.*[4] By this new *conversi* institute Abbot William brought into the monastery the former hired servant, raised him to the religious state, admitted him to the choir and the cloister, and clothed him as a lay brother with the habit of the other monks.[5]

Thus there are seen for the first time two separate and distinct classes of religious within the same monastery; on the one hand the *conversi,* the former hired servants, who had been raised from the lay to the religious state, and on the other, the lettered monks (*literati*), and among these also any who might happen to be clerics.

Be it noted that Blessed William legislated only for the *conversi laici* (hired servants) already connected with the monastery; he did not purposely introduce lay brothers as auxiliaries to enable the monks to live a life more in conformity with their rule. This feature was left to be added by the religious orders of the Middle Ages.[6]

2. *Development in the Cistercian and Later Orders*

It was the Cistercians, the Church's first centralized religious order, who obtained the initial papal approval of the lay brother

---

[3] Cf. Heimbucher, I, 204.

[4] Cf. Deroux, *Les Origines de l'Oblature bénédictine,* "Les Editions de la Revue Mabillon," I (Viénne: Abbaye Saint-Martin de Ligugé, 1927), p. 95.

[5] *Consuetudines Hirsaugienses,* Lib. I, c. 33-*MPL,* CL, 966; *ibid.,* Lib. I, c. 49—*MPL,* CL, 979; *Observationes Praviae* n. 5—*MPL,* CL, 892-893.

[6] Cf. Brockhaus, *Religious Who are Known as Conversi,* The Catholic University of America Canon Law Studies, n. 225 (Washington, D. C.: The Catholic University of America Press, 1946), p. 15.

institute. It was in this Order that it grew to its greatest development.[7] When the founders of Citeaux introduced lay brothers into their monasteries, they did it as part of their reformative program. They hoped that this class of lay religious would permit the Cistercian monks to keep their Rule perfectly. Hence, their economic purpose was subordinate to their ultimate ascetic one, and it was the labor of the *conversi* that made it possible for the other monks to lead a balanced Benedictine life, free from solicitude for material necessities. "These *conversi* whom we need as helpers we receive into our care as we do monks, and we consider them as much our brothers and partakers in our spiritual and temporal goods as the monks." [8]

The first written synthetic and detailed Rule for *conversi* or lay brothers was composed by the Cistercian monks early in the twelfth century. This Rule, which consisted of twenty-two chapters, was entitled *Usus Conversorum.*[9] A monk of Clairvaux added to this the *Regula Conversorum*, which served as a supplement to the *Usus* and contained sixteen chapters.[10]

In the General Chapter of this Order held in 1220 the Capitular Fathers decreed:

> In receptione conversum ista sit consideratio, ut solo victu contentus antequam vestiatur, *sex mensibus serviat in habitu saeculari,* et tunc si utilis invenitur, tonsoretur, et probationem faciat in Ordine consuetam, nisi talis sit persona, quam pro evitando periculo illis sex mensibus oporteat non probari.[11] (Writer's Italics).

This statute of the General Chapter makes it strikingly evident that the special legislation requiring some form of a postulancy

---

[7] Cf. Hoffmann, *Das Konverseninstitut des Cisterzienserordens in seinem Ursprung und seiner Organisation,* Freiburger historische Studien, I (Freiburgi, Br., 1905) (hereafter cited *Das Konverseninstitut*).

[8] *Inst. Cap. Gen. collecta anno 1134,* c. 8—Guignard, *Les monuments primitifs de la Règle cisterciénne publiés d'après les manuscrits de l'Abbaye de Cîteaux,* Analecta Divionensia, X (Dijon, 1878), p. 251.

[9] Hoffmann, *Das Konverseninstitut,* p. 48.

[10] Martène-Durand, *Thesaurus,* IV, 1647 ff.

[11] *Statuta Anni MCCXX*—Martène-Durand, *Thesaurus,* IV, 1327, n. 2.

was almost as old as the *conversi* institute itself. As had been the case, however, with so many other Rules and constitutions which demanded a time of initial probation, the superior was here too empowered, in particular cases, to dispense from this requirement, if he prudently judged that the candidate was of sufficiently high moral caliber that this probationary period could be safely waived. It is interesting to note that this Rule required a six-month postulancy for the *conversi*, the same period that is now obligatory for them by the common law.

The Cistercian model was not an isolated phenomenon, but it portrayed the lay brother institute in its full development. It served as an exemplar for much of the later legislation of the Canons Regular[12] and the Carthusians.[13]

By 1132 the laybrotherhood of Citeaux received the equivalent approval of the papacy through the privilege of exemption granted to it by Pope Innocent II, and by the dawn of the thirteenth century it had spread throughout Christendom, along with the Order itself.

The Mendicants adopted this same fundamental principle for their Orders with the exception that, instead of enabling their monks to live according to their Rule, it was the function of the lay brothers to take upon themselves such tasks and cares as might hinder their clerical confrères in their apostolic work.[14]

While it is true that in dealing with the *conversi* institute one can not draw general conclusions from particular legislation, for there is in fact no homogeneous "*conversi* institute," nevertheless, it seems safe to conclude that in most of the orders where this institute did exist there was required from its very inception some form of preliminary probation. This probationary period, in orders which followed most closely the model of the Cistercians, was

---

[12] Cf. *Constitutiones Praemonstratensium et Consuetudines Canonicorum Regularium S. Victoris Parisiensis*—Martène, *De Antiquis Ecclesiae Ritibus* (Ed. novissima, 4 vols., Antverpiae-Venetiis, 1763-1764), III, 323 ff; 741ff.

[13] Knowles, *The Monastic Order in England* (Cambridge: University Press, 1941), pp. 378-379.

[14] Cf. Mulhern, *The Early Dominican Lay Brother* (Washington, 1944).

frequently of six months' duration. But this was purely a matter of special law, which was left to the individual Rule and constitutions to determine. Indeed, there are examples where no previous probation was required, as was the case with the early Dominican lay brother, of whom there was demanded merely a six-month novitiate.[15]

3. *Papal Legislation*

One would search the papal registers and the collections of papal decrees from the eleventh to the twentieth century in vain, if one were looking for an express pronouncement of the Holy See in regard to the postulancy. The simple truth of the matter is that such a pronouncement does not exist. For the postulancy was always an institute of special law, and the Roman Pontiffs were perfectly content to leave the regulating of this initial period of probation, if indeed it existed at all, to the competent superiors of the individual orders.

There is, however, a Constitution of Pope Clement VIII, *Cum ad regularem*, of the 19th of March, 1603, from which one may deduce that it was the mind of the Pope that there should be some form of a brief and previous probationary period, even for lay brothers. The section of this decree which is to our purpose stated:

> (The Superiors) are to take care that all candidates, inculding *conversi*, be instructed, by those whose duty it is, regarding the Rule they are to profess, the three essential vows, the religious state, and the particular regulations and constitutions of the respective Order, before they are admitted to the regular habit.[16]

---

[15] Cf. Mulhern, *The Early Dominican Lay Brother.*

[16] Provideant quoque, ut omnes etiam Conversi recipiendi, priusquam ad habitum regularem admittantur, ab iis quibus munus hoc incumbit, de regula quam professuri sunt, tribus votis essentialibus, statuque Regulari, et aliis cuiusque Ordinis peculiaribus institutis, et Constitutionibus diligenter instruantur."—*Codicis Iuris Canonici Fontes,* cura Emi Petri Card. Gasparri editi (9 vols., Romae [Postea Civitate Vaticana]: Typis Polyglottis Vaticanis, 1923-1939; Vols. VII-IX ed. cura et studio Emi Iustiniani Card. Serédi), I, n. 189, p. 358 (hereafter cited *Fontes*).

In the introduction of the *Cum ad regularem* the Pope stated that there is nothing more conducive to the relaxation of regular discipline than negligence in testing and examining the spirit of candidates for the religious life in order to see if it is truly from God and an especial desire of serving Him, and carelessness in the further education and instruction of these same candidates. In order, therefore, to counteract these dangers to the regular discipline, the Pope set down a number of regulations on these points which he made obligatory for the superiors.[17] Among the rules which Pope Clement VIII commanded to be observed was that which has been quoted above.

Although it is quite evident that the Holy Father did not mention the postulancy by name in this document, nevertheless he seemed certainly to have had it in mind, for the purposes of the brief period of instruction which he commanded before the reception of the habit, and those of the postulancy are identical, namely, the previous testing of the aspirant and the imparting of instruction to him in the fundamentals of the religious life.

While this Constitution has been quoted here with special reference to the postulancy as demanded for lay brothers, it must be

---

[17] *Cum ad regularem,* §§ 1, 2:

"§1. Cum ad Regularem disciplinam in singulis Religiosorum Monasteriis propagandam, Novitiorum institutio maxime utilis sit, ac necessaria, et nihil ad gravem illam, ac laudatissimam priscorum Patrum vivendi rationem relaxandam, maiorem vim habuisse compertum sit, quam vel nimiam in recipiendis Novitiis facilitatem supra numerum, quem capere, atque alere Monasteria ipsa possent, vel negligentiam in probando, et examinando eorum spiritu, an vere esset ex Deo, atque ex praecipuo desiderio illi inserviendi, vel denique incuriam in eis educandis, atque instituendis.

"§2. Idcirco, ut huiusmodi incommodo deinceps occurratur, praecipitur omnibus, et singulis, ad quos spectat, ut in recipiendis Novitiis, et in eorum institutione atque educatione, nec non in Magistri, et aliorum Ministrorum electione, praeter alia, quae in sacris Canonibus, ac decretis, praesertim Concilii Tridentini, Pontificiis, et cuiuscumque Ordinis, aut Instituti Constitutionibus continentur, tam in alias designatis, quam nunc, et imposterum ad hoc designandis Monasteriis, et Conventibus, haec, quae sequuntur, inviolate observari, et exequi perpetuo curent."—*Fontes,* I, n. 189.

kept in mind that it applied with equal force to all other religious as well, as is evident from a reading of the document. There will be occasion to refer to this papal pronouncement again in the discussion of the necessity of a postulancy for clerical religious.

In a decree dated September 21, 1624, the Sacred Congregation of the Council renewed the whole Constitution *Cum ad regularem.*[18]

The final piece of pre-Code legislation for the postulancy with regard to the *conversi* was enacted in the decree *Sacrosancta* of the Sacred Congregation for Religious, dated January 1, 1911.[19]

This decree was the first and the only piece of general pre-Code legislation which expressly required that all *conversi*, before their entrance into the novitiate, had first to undergo a period of preliminary probation. The reason that motivated the Sacred Congregation to issue this decree was, no doubt, the large number of requests that it was receiving to dispense lay brothers from their solemn vows. Inasmuch as the decree itself incorporates a complete exposition of the facts as seen by the Sacred Congregation, parts of it are here translated by the writer in full:

> The Holy Church of God has seen fit to permit religious Orders to have solemn vows, so that those observing the evangelical counsels in these Orders should belong to a state more stable in Christian society both in acknowledgment and in effect. The Church admits even those not destined to share in the priesthood of Christ, namely the *conversi* or lay brothers, to these solemn vows.
>
> Since, however, by solemn vows a man is bound to the divine service by a wholly irrevocable, strict and public bond before the Church and all the faithful, it is most fitting that those who have thus pledged themselves forever to follow more closely in the footsteps of Christ persevere faithful to their promise. This is especially to be noted regarding the lay brothers or *conversi*, who cause wonderment and scandal among the faithful when the latter see them return to the world after solemn profession, engaging in secular business like other men, with no further relation to the life they led in religion.
>
> The spirit of the times, however, which unhappily guaran-

[18] *Fontes,* n. 2454.

[19] *Fontes,* n. 4407.

tees undue liberty to men, has filtered also into the sacred precincts of the monasteries. This spirit has weakened the good will to persevere along with the desire of leading a humble life, hidden in Christ, such as is demanded of *conversi* in monasteries, especially in those lay brothers who perhaps have entered religion more out of necessity than of their own free will, or those whom superiors have received without due caution, or those who have abused the gifts God gave them. Holy Mother Church, choosing the lesser of two evils, has sometimes in her great mercy permitted them to depart. . . .

That the dignity of the vows, then, which lay brothers also promise solemnly, continue to be held in the honor that it deserves in the Church, and in order the better to insure the sacred pledge of a vocation in our most difficult times, this Sacred Congregation, in whose charge rest the affairs of religious societies, has considered the matter most diligently in the Lord upon exploring the reasons and causes, and proposing the means and remedies. It has asked the opinion of the highest superiors of the great Orders and that of many of its consultors. Considering all these things diligently, the Eminent Cardinals of this Congregation in a plenary session of July 29, 1910, decided to lay down certain rules to be observed in the future regarding the admission of lay religious, their initial training, their subsequent education, and their final pronouncing of vows.

The following rules are therefore to be observed by all religious communities in which solemn vows are taken also by the *conversi*, namely:

1. The superiors general have the faculty to permit provincial superiors in particular cases to receive young men who wish to become lay brothers even when they have not as yet completed their seventeenth year. All other provisions of the law are to be observed when such permission is granted.

2. No one is to be admitted to the novitiate until he has *completed a postulancy of at least two years*, or even more if the constitutions so prescribe, under penalty of the invalidity of his subsequent profession. (Writer's Italics).

3. The novitiate is not to be started before the twenty-first year, according to the law now in force, and it is to last one or even two years, according to the constitutions of the respective Order.

4. After the novitiate, with all other prescriptions properly fulfilled, lay religious can be admitted to simple vows. While

these vows are taken as perpetual on the part of the religious, their juridical consequences will bind the Order for a period of six years.

5. When six years have been spent in simple vows, and with the completion of the thirtieth year of age, and not before, under penalty of invalidity, and only when all the other provisions of the law have been duly observed, may lay religious be admitted to solemn vows.

6. The prescrpitions regarding simple and solemn vows as enacted in the preceding articles are to be observed also by the lay brothers now living in the monasteries, if they have not as yet made their solemn profession.

This long period of nine years, it is hoped, will enable superiors to ascertain the constancy of their subjects, and will give the subjects an opportunity to acquire a thorough knowledge of the life they intend to embrace with solemn vows, so that they can do this after being more firmly grounded in virtue and more richly endowed with a mature judgment.

This should give some hope of later perseverance, but even this hope will not be entirely trustworthy unless there be employed, together with similar helps, the following precautions and safeguards, which the Holy See has strongly recommended through the centuries, and which the better disciplined religious societies have found successful in practice.

In the first place, the admission of prospective *conversi* is to follow only after the making of many and diligent inquiries, and the employment of all due cautions. The provincial superior must learn whether the candidate is of legitimate birth, of good morals, of high regard among the people, whether he has the proper docility of a recruit in religion, and especially whether he is moved by the right kind of motive in embracing the religious state. For there are many who seem to enter religion to seek after a soft life rather than to leave it, who seek "in the monastery what they could not afford outside" (*Reg. S. Augustini*, c. I, 3)[20] or who want to lead an easy life which is free from cares, unworthy of the honor shown it. . . . These indeed are religious in garb only, and not in virtue, and they would have done better to walk the broad ways of the world than to endanger perhaps their eternal salvation by pretending to things above them.

Only those who have been found worthy after even secret

---

[20] *MPL*, XXXIII, 960, where this statement occurs in *Epistola CCXI*, n. 5.

investigations, and who are well recommended in the light of the documents furnished, *are to be admitted to the postulancy,* with the customary permission of the major superiors. (Writer's Italics).

"It has been sufficiently demonstrated," says Clement VIII in his instruction for the reception and education of novices, *Cum ad regularem,* §15, "that the perfect education of *conversi* brings honor and glory to the religious state, and gives a useful and edifying example to the faithful." It is necessary therefore that from the very beginning the religious spirit and that of their Order pervade their whole soul. . . .

For this purpose, a father, recommended by the maturity of his years and the manner of his life, *is to be placed over the postulants.* (Writer's Italics).

A beginning often has to be made with a teaching of the very rudiments of civility, as candidates for the lay brotherhood often come from among the less privileged. Boorishness in manners and speech, in walking and eating, is to be gradually but in the end thoroughly rooted out. A soiled garb, when it is not worn for the love of humility and the contempt of the world, but rather because of uncouth negligence, does not savor of the spirit of Christ, and therefore does not augur well for the man who wears it. Personal cleanliness and neatness in dress, always with due modesty and simplicity, are to be greatly cultivated. The ordinary rules of politeness which an urbane education postulates for social conduct should be also observed in the monasteries, as fraternal charity demands, for the charitable man avoids annoying his neighbors. The rudeness of those who seek only their own pleasure, to the neglect of others, is found to be irksome to the brethren and to give them plenty of opportunity for exercising their patience.

This external discipline will lead to a proper character development, imparting a noble delicacy of spirit which avoids every least offense to others, which anticipates their wishes, and which shows a habitual pleasant disposition, preferring others to self.

It is important, however, that Christian charity vivify, rule and ennoble these various actions, so that whatever is praiseworthy and pleasing to others in our words, deeds and forebearance proceed from a heart filled with charity.

If all these things are befitting in a lay religious, they must all the more stand out in the priests, and in the clerics who are destined for the priesthood, so that through the contemplation of the example of those who are above them the *conversi* may be led along the path not only of virtue, but also of courtesy and politeness.

Thus, by instruction, encouragement, patience and especially by example, it will not be hard to raise the manners and habits of the more uncouth to a culture and grace that will soon after their entrance into religion justify the application of these words of St. Bernard to them: "They have clothed themselves with a chastened mien and deportment, they have adorned their bodily bearing with graceful poise and gravity . . . a greater moderation of speech, a happier expression of face, a more modest appearance in company, a more sedate manner of life. . . . ." (*Sermo* 63, *in Cant.*, n. 6).[21]

That the spiritual training may produce these fruits should be the whole ambition *of the superior of the postulants* and the master of novices. These directors should make it their pride and duty . . . to promote the progress of the lay brothers in the way of holiness. (Writer's Italics).

In accord with the decrees of the Holy See, they shall explain all of the Christian doctrine, and especially what pertains to the proper and fruitful reception of the sacraments of Penance and Holy Communion, using as their guide the Catechism of the Council of Trent for pastors. At the same time they shall teach them the obligations they will assume at religious profession and the virtues they must cultivate to lead the life of the vows. Likewise they shall explain the parts of the Rule and the constitutions which pertain to the *conversi.*

Conferences or sermons shall be given to the lay brothers on specified days, not only to the juniors, but to all, including the seniors in profession and in years. The content-matter of these sermons or conferences shall deal with the catechism, with the counsels of the spiritual life, with an explanation of the Rule and constitutions, but also with the practical norms and examples of a modest and composed refinement of manners. . . .

All these presents having been brought before His Holiness Pope Pius X, he has deigned to approve and ratify them, everything to the contrary notwithstanding, even though it be deserving of special mention.[22]

---

[21] *MPL,* CLXXXIII, 1083.

[22] S.C. de Religiosis, decr. *Sacrosancta,* 1 ian. 1911—*AAS,* III (1911), 29-39.

Certainly this papal document is so complete in itself that it will not need much comment. It should, however, be pointed out that this document was meant only for the lay brothers who took solemn vows and had no effect on any other class of religious, clerical or lay. Likewise this is the first and the only decree of the Holy See that ever mentioned the postulancy as being required under pain of the invalidity of the subsequent profession of vows.

As is evident from the parts of the decree quoted above, the pre-Code common law required a postulancy of at least two years, or even longer, if the constitutions of a particular institute so prescribed, for all lay brothers who would eventually make solemn profession.

Since in the first rule set down in the decree *Sacrosancta* it was allowed to provincial superiors so authorized by the superior general to admit candidates to the lay brotherhood before they had completed their seventeenth year, and since in the third rule it was stated that they were not to commence their novitiate before they were twenty-one years of age, it seems obvious that at least some of the candidates for the lay brotherhood spent more than four years as postulants.

There is no indication that the two-year period, or the longer time which might be required by a particular set of constitutions, had to be computed mathematically, or that it had to be continuous. With the permission of the superior and for a just cause, the postulant could remain some days outside the religious house to which he was assigned. A moral union of the time was of course necessary.[23] The exact computation of the time of the postulancy was not treated by the authors prior to the Code.[24]

This decree of te Holy See was in addition quite explicit in its requirement that there be placed over the postulants a mature

---

[23] Balzer, *The Computation of Time in a Canonical Novitiate,* The Catholic University of America Canon Law Studies, n. 212 (Washington, D. C.: The Catholic University of America Press, 1945), p. 76.

[24] Battandier, *Guide Canonique pour les Constitutions des Instituts à Voeux Simples* (6. ed., Paris: Gabalda, 1923), pp. 94-97 (hereafter cited *Guide Canonique*); Piat, *Praelectiones Juris Regularis* (ed. Victorius ab Appeltern, 3.ed., 2 vols., Tornaci, 1906), I, 82-83.

father whose life was outstanding for his practice of virtue. It was not left to the individual superior to decide what training the postulant should receive, but in most specific terms it was indicated what the exact nature of this training and education should be.

The doctrine of this decree *Sacrosancta*, which from 1911 onward to the enactment of the present Code was the basic general law for *conversi* postulants who were eventually to take solemn vows, was in part abrogated and in part retained by the present Code.

B. Later Development of a Postulancy for Clerical Religious

From all that has been said previously concerning the postulancy, it will be immediately evident that this institute was at least not too obscurely prefigured in the short period of probation which from the very beginning of the organized forms of religious life was demanded by the monastic lawgivers of both the East and the West.[25]

Relative to this probation there was no distinction between clerical and non-clerical monks. The so-called postulancy was required equally for both, unless the superior deemed it prudent to dispense from this regulation in the case of a priest or a well-known layman seeking admission to the monastery.

This salutary practice of requiring a short period of probation for all candidates, even such as were distined for the reception of Sacred Orders, before their actual entrance into the novitiate was continued by the legislators for the Clerks Regular. In these institutes the candidates were first to be received for a few days as guests.

The Rule of the Society of Jesus, founded by St. Ignatius Loyola and approved on September 27, 1540, contained the following section entitled *Regulae Magistri Novitiorum*:

> Postquam in Domino statuetur, ad probationem aliquem admittendum esse in domo, vel habitatione separata primae probationis; *hospitum more duodecim dies, vel usque ad viginti,*

[25] Cf. *supra*, pp. 4-24.

> *et amplius (prout Superiori videbitur), diversetur;* ut eo tempore de iis, quae pertinent ad Societatem, ipse certior reddatur, et Societas eundem plenius in Domino cognoscat.[26] (Writer's Italics).

In the Rule of the Piarist Order, founded by St. Josephus Calasanctius in 1617, there was the following directive:

> Admittendi per examen approbati *tanquam hospites, per aliquot dies in domo probationis collocentur;* ut illle vicissim Institutum, illos Institutum probet.[27] (Writer's Italics).

The more ancient congregations of men religious also recognized the utility of such a period of initial probation, and often required it of those seeking admittance to their ranks. For example, the Rule of the Redemptorists, founded on November 9, 1732, by St. Alphonsus Liguori and canonically approved by Pope Benedict XIV in 1749, contained the following directive:

> Ita suscepti *per aliquod tempus in propriis vestibus probabuntur* et, factis per dies quindecim exercitiis spiritualibus, in novitiatum admittentur. . . .[28] (Writer's Italics).

While these Rules and constitutions have been quoted here for what they were, merely examples of the special law, they nevertheless serve to show that a requisite period of probation was quite widespread, and even obligatory for the class of clerical religious.

All the legislation that existed on this point was of a purely private nature, and nowhere is there to be found any general law which demanded this previous trial for clerical religious, or for that matter until 1911 for any class of religious. However, the papal Constitution of Pope Clement VIII, *Cum ad regularem,* of March 19, 1603, to which reference has been previously made,[29] seemed beyond a doubt, apart from the lack of an express mention

---

[26] *Regulae Magistri Novitiorum,* n. 9; Cf. *Exam. gen.,* c. I, § 13; *Const.* p. I, c. IV, pars. 1 et 2.

[27] *Constitutiones Religionis Clericorum Regularium Pauperum Matris Dei Scholarum Piarum,* p. 1, c. III (II, III).

[28] *Codex Regularum et Constitutionum Congregationis SS. Redemptoris,* p. 3, c. II, n. III.

[29] Cf. *supra,* pp. 30-32.

of the postulancy, to contemplate some period of probation. This papal pronouncement contained the following instruction to superiors:

> (The superiors) are to take care that all candidates, including *conversi*, be instructed, by those whose duty it is, regarding the Rule they are to profess, the three essential vows, the religious state, and the particular regulations and constitutions of the respective Order, before they are admitted to the regular habit.[30]

It cannot be claimed that the Holy Father made it obligatory for all religious Orders thenceforward to subject their prospective members to a postulancy. The most that can be claimed it that there was required some previous instruction of the candidate with regard to the Rule, the vows of religion, the religious state in general and the particular constitutions of the institute in question. Certainly a convenient way for superiors to put this directive into operation was to require of all aspirants a time of initial probation and instruction similar to our modern institute of the postulancy. But the Pope said nothing concerning the way in which this mandate was to be carried out. It was left, as were most of the matters pertaining to the religious life, to the prudence and discretion of the superiors of the various Orders to find the most apt means to make this directive operative. If the constitutions of a particular institute already had made some provision for this point, then this law did not apply to it. If they did not contain such a provision, then the superiors to whom this pertained were to see to it that such a provision was inserted. As was mentioned above, the most convenient way in which this requirement of a previous time of observation and instruction could be carried out was to demand of all candidates a period of initial probation, corresponding in nature and purpose, if not in name, to our present-day postulancy.

This is all that can be said for the canonical postulancy as required for clerical religious before the Code, for so the law stood until the promulgation of the Code. Besides this canonical postulancy, however, there is also another postulancy referred to by authors as a postulancy in the broad sense of the term. This

[30] *Fontes,* I, n. 189, p. 358.

postulancy, which had its origin in France, around the end of the eighteenth century, will be treated briefly in the following chapter of this work.

C. Postulancy as Required for Nuns

1. *Early Legislation*

All that has been said previously about the laws concerning the postulancy in Orders of men religious applies with equal vigor, *mutatis mutandis*, to the nuns of the second Order, who followed the same Rule as the monks.

Those nuns also who did not belong to any of the second Orders but who constituted independent monasteries, sometimes only of diocesan approval, did or did not require a period of previous probation for their prospective members, according as the constitutions so provided. An example of such an independent institution of nuns (that is, independent of any first Order of men religious) is the Sisters of the Visitation, whose Constitutions, drawn up by St. Francis de Sales, contained the following directives about this point.

Constitution XLIII

> Of the First Reception of Those Who Wish to be Admitted into the Community.
>
> No maiden may enter into the Community who has not completed her fifteenth year, and who cannot read, if she presents herself to become a choir sister, and who does not manifest a great desire of Christian perfection. . . .
>
> And when any maiden or woman is proposed for reception, she shall before all things be made to come to the House, *where she shall stay some days as a stranger*, that she may be seen and considered by the superior and the sisters. (Writer's Italics).
>
> And when the superior thinks the time is come for it, she shall make the postulant ask for her admission in full Chapter; and then she shall take the votes of all the sisters, and if the superior, with the majority of the sisters, agrees to receive her, she shall be admitted to the *first probation*; having first taken the advice of the Spiritual Father, who on his part shall enquire into the circumstances of the postulant, that he

may the better advise the sisters on the occasion.... (Writer's Italics).

Constitution XLIV

Of the Admission of Novices

The postulant being assured of her reception may, when the superior appoints, make the first trial in her secular dress,. which she shall continue to wear *for at least six months* to make trial and to consider whether she will be able to adapt herself to the Rules and observances of the Congregation, which she shall now be made to practice exactly: and she shall be made to understand that the Congregation is a school of abnegation of self, of mortification of the senses, of resignation of all acts of the human will: and in short a Mount Calvary, where, with Jesus Christ, His chaste spouses ought to be spiritually crucified, in order to be glorified with Him hereafter. And, meanwhile, they shall bid her prepare by meditations and prayers to make a general confession if the confessor thinks it advisable. (Writer's Italics).

While still a postulant the superior or the mistress to whose care she is confided shall study her character, her inclinations, humours and passions, the better to correct her faults, cultivate her qualities and thus direct her towards the perfection which she ought to acquire in the Congregation.

The appointed time being over, the votes shall be taken, and if they are favorable, she shall prepare herself, and the novice's habit shall be given her.[31]

Again it must be remembered that these quoted parts of the foregoing Constitutions serve simply as an example of what was required by way of special law. What was said of the postulancy in general was equally applicable to this institute in regard to the monasteries of nuns, namely, there was no general legislation on the matter. Any laws which existed were of a purely specific character, as found in the Rules and constitutions of the various individual institutes.

But it seems a safe conclusion that most, if not all, of the constitutions demanded some form of preliminary probation and trial whose purpose corresponded exactly to the modern institute of the postulancy.

[31] *Constitutions of the Sisters of the Visitation after the Original Manuscripts* (London: Manresa Press, 1930), XLIII, XLIV, pp. 206-211.

In proof of this statement one may point to a particular rescript which allowed a monastery of nuns to admit its postulants within the confines of the papal cloister during the time of their probation. For example, there is a rescript from the Sacred Congregation of Bishops and Regulars on this point under date of May 8, 1906, which runs as follows:

> Beatissime Pater
>
> Episcopus Auriensis, ad pedes S.V. provolutus, exponit quae sequuntur:
>
> Mos invaluit in conventu monialium S. Francisci oppidi vulgo Allariz, huius dioecesis, ut postulantes priusquam habitum accipiant, probationis periodum peragant intra claustra monasterii commorando, quin in scriptis ullam licentiam a S. Sede obtinuerint, neque postulaverint. Episcopus orator iuri clausurae papalis, cuius est custos, prospiciens et tranquillitati monialium consulendo, petit a S.V. licentiam in scriptis competentem ut quaecumque habitum monialium in hoc monasterio accepturae sunt, nomine et tituulo postulantium, intra claustra degere et commorari possint per probationis periodum. Et Deus.
>
> Vigore specialium facultatum a SSmo Domino Nostro concessarum, Sacra Congregatio Emorum S.R.E. Cardinalium negotiis et consultationibus Episcoporum et Regularium praeposita benigne annuit precibus Episcopi oratoris pro petita facultate ad quinquennium. Contrariis quibuscumque non obstatibus. Romae, 8 Maii 1906.[32]

Hence it seems that it was more or less the common pre-Code practice for nuns to require some manner of initial probation before they granted admission to a prospective aspirant to the religious life. If this period of trial was to be spent within the cloister, there was required the further permission of the Holy See, given either directly or through its delegate.

2. *Papal Legislation*

As there was only one document of the Holy See with the force of common law which demanded a postulancy for *conversi* who eventually were to take solemn vows, so too, there was but one

[32] *ASS*, XL (1906), 71-72.

similar common law papal document that required a postulancy in monasteries of nuns with solemn vows.

This was the decree *Quo propositum,* issued by the Sacred Congregation for Religious on the 15th of August, 1912, the full text of which is here reproduced:

> Decretum de Postulatu in Monasteriis Votorum Solemnium
>
> Quo propositum vitae religiosae perpetuo profitendae melius exploretur, et dignitati status religiosi uberius consulatur, imminutis, in quantum fieri possit, defectionibus, Emi ac Rmi Patres Cardinales Sacrae Congregationis de Religiosis, in plenariis comitiis ad Vaticanum habitis die 2 Augusti, 1912, sequentia statuerunt, nempe:
>
> 1. Quaelibet Postulans in monasteriis votorum solemnium et clausurae papalis poterit admitti, sine praevia S. Sedes venia, servata tamen aliis de iure servandis.
>
> 2. Quaelibet Postulans, antequam Novitiatum ingrediatur, probanda erit per tempus, et iuxta modum, in propriis cuiusvis Monasterii Constitutionibus praescriptum.
>
> 3. Si nihil in istis quoad haec statuatur, tunc probatio facienda est saltem per sex menses, ita tamen, ut Postulantes, intra septa Monasterii, probationis causa, admissae, utantur veste modesti coloris, diversa ab habitu Ordinis, quem non induant, nisi quando Novitiatum proprie dictum inchoaturae sint.
>
> Facta autem de his omnibus fideli relatione Sanctissimo Domino Nostro Pio Papae X per infrascriptum Sacrae Congregationis Secretarium die 5 Augusti, 1912, Sanctitas Sua eadem approbare et confirmare dignita est. Contrariis non obstantibus quibuscumque.
>
> Datum Romae, ex Secretaria Sacrae Congregationis de Religiosis, die 15 Augusti 1912.[33]

From the above quoted decree of the Holy See it is readily apparent that the Sacred Congregation of Religious considered the postulancy as a safeguard for the stability of the religious state, for the protection of the professed members, and for the aspirants themselves, and as providing an adequate time of probation and preparation before recruits in religion were to be admitted to the

[33] *AAS,* IV (1912), 565-566; *Fontes,* n. 4412.

profession of vows. This papal pronouncement also bears out what has been repeated in this work so often, that is, that until this point in the history of religious institutions the postulancy was or was not demanded for candidates in accord simply with the regulations of the individual constitutions. Even with the issuing of this decree the Holy See did not entirely depart from this principle, for the constitutions were still to be the determining factor in regard to the postulancy as long as they required one. If a particular set of constitutions happened to be silent on this point of an initial probationary period, then this decree required that a postulancy of at least six months be instituted. It seems from the wording used in this document that, if the constitutions of a certain institute were less stringent than the decree *Quo propositum* in their demands for the postulancy, for example, by requiring only a three-month postulancy, then these constitutions were to be followed.

It should be noted also that the postulancy as required for nuns was not mentioned in the decree as essential for the validity of their subsequent profession, as was the case with the postulancy demanded for *conversi*. This requirement for validity could, of course, have been insisted upon by the constitutions.

This papal law was also explicit on several other points in regard to the postulants, namely, that they could be admitted within the papal cloister without the previous permission of the Apostolic See, which had been required until then, and that the postulants inside the cloister for their probation were not necessarily to wear a uniform, but were in any case to be modestly clothed, not, however, in the habit of the novices.

On May 29, 1913, the same Sacred Congregation of Religious communicated to the Bishop of Havana the following rules, which were to serve at least as directive norms:

> 1. The postulants may and should assist at all of the community acts which pertain to the external religious discipline, with the exception of recreation, and, if possible, the community meals.
>
> 2. They are to be subject to the direction of the mistress of novices (in the supposition that they live in the house of

the novitiate) who may, if necessary, choose from among the other senior sisters an assistant who will aid her in the instruction of the postulants.

3. The postulants are not to be assigned to all the offices which the other religious perform, but only to those which harmonize perfectly with the separation of the postulants from the rest of the community.[34]

While this communication of the Sacred Congregation must be regarded as a purely private decree, it is, nevertheless, indicative as to what was the mind of the Holy See on certain points of the religious discipline as they affected the postulants.

It seems that, if the constitutions were silent on the appointment of a religious to be in charge of the postulants, this office fell to the mistress of novices, at least in the house of the novitiate.

In regard to the law of the cloister as it bound postulants, there is the following response of the Sacred Congregation of Religious under date of November 7, 1916:

Dubia circa egressum postulantium e monasteriis monialium.

Sacrae Congregationi de Religiosis sequentia dubia, pro opportuna solutione, proposita sunt:

I. An puellae postulantes e monasteriis clausurae papali subiectis egredi possint, parentes vel notos invisendi gratia, aut alia de causa.

Et quatenus negative:

II. Utrum ad huiusmodi egressum venia Apostolicae Sedis indigeant, an satis sit consensus Ordinarii.

Eadem S. Congregatio, re mature perpensa, respondendum censuit:

Ad I. Negative.

Ad II. Affirmative ad primam partem; negative ad secundam.

Datum Romae, ex Secretaria eiusdem S. Congregationis de Religiosis, die 7 novembris 1916.[35]

It is evident from this response of the Sacred Congregation that

[34] *Del Boletin Oficial Eclesiastico de la Habana de 30 julio de 1913*, pp. 157-158—Jardi, *El Derecho de las Religiosas* (2.ed., Vich: Editorial Serafico, 1927), pp. 217-218.

[35] *AAS*, VIII (1916), 446.

postulants were to be held by the strict law of the papal cloister. They, like any of the professed nuns, were not to leave the enclosure without the permission of the Holy See. As was seen earlier, this permission of the Holy See was not required for their admission after the issuance of the decree *Quo propositum.*

This was the pre-Code law for the postulancy as required for nuns, much of which the Code has retained and made binding on all for whom a postulancy is now demanded by way of a common norm.

D. Postulancy as Required for Women Religious in Congregations

1. *Early Legislation*

Special law began to introduce a canonical postulancy, properly so called, for sisters in congregations during the second half of the last century. The Sacred Congregation of Bishops and Regulars by its repeated animadversions, slowly but clearly, made known its mind on such points as the time, the place and other essentials of the postulancy, for this class of religious.

In the beginning the postulancy in these congregations depended upon the will of the superior general, who more or less prolonged this time of trial as she thought prudent, depending upon the acceptability and disposition of each individual candidate. As is quite understandable, however, this manner of procedure left the way open to difficulties and inconveniences. Superiors sometimes kept their candidates too long in the postulancy, and then sent them back to their families upon judging them not apt for the life of the community. The Sacred Congregation wished to put an end to such difficulties, and accordingly resolved to fix a maximum as well as a minimum time limit for this period of first probation. This Congregation on May 12, 1897, stated that there must be determined not only a minimum but also a maximum length of time for the postulancy.[36]

[36] S. C. Ep. et Reg., *Annecien.*, 12 maii 1897, ad 4um (Sorores S. Joseph) —Battandier, *Guide Canonique*, p. 95.

But the constitutions of institutes whose members were professed with simple vows did not sufficiently determine or fix this time limit, and thus there remained too great a margin for arbitrary action on the part of the superiors. It was possible for superiors to choose the two terms of the maximum and the minimum time of the postulancy in such a way that the goal after which the Sacred Congregation was striving could not be attained. Therefore, after a period of some uncertainty, it was decided that the postulancy should last for at least six months. "Expediens erit statuere quod probatio postulatium ante illarum ingressum in novitiatum non sit minor sex mensibus." [37]

Then there was established a maximum time beyond which the constitutions could not make any demand, and after the completion of which the candidate was either to be admitted to the novitiate or sent back to her family. With the minimum time of the postulancy duly fixed, the constitutions could allow the superior in particular cases to prolong this probation, but only for a predetermined length of time which precluded all further prorogation. The 1901 *Normae* especially in n. 65, modified this legislation, as will presently be seen.

As soon as the time of the postulancy was over the aspirant was either to be admitted to the novitiate or sent home. This the Sacred Congregation stated in express terms when it granted permission to an Institute to prolong the postulancy for a period of two months. "Experiantur autem postulantes per sex integros menses, vel iustis gravibus de causis concurrentibus, per octo ad summum, quibus expletis, aut ad habitum admittantur, aut dimittantur." [38]

The postulancy was to last for the minimufm time fixed by the constitutions. If an exception were to be made in favor of the superioress for shortening the time of the postulancy for any candidate about whose life she had intimate first-hand information, it certainly seems that exception should have been applicable for

---

[37] S. C. Ep. et Reg., *Barcinonen.*, 16 nov. 1888, ad 14 (Animad. in Const. Sororum Tertii Ordinis Capuccinarum Divinae Pastorae)—Battandier, *loc. cit.*

[38] S. C. Ep. et Reg., *Gratianopolitan.*, 28 sept. 1892, ad 3um (Parvae Sorores Operarii)—Battandier, *ibid.*, p. 97.

those young ladies who had been educated in the houses of the institute in question, and who were consequently well known to the superior and to the other sisters. But even in this case it was not allowed to the superior to dispense from the time set down by the constitutions. "Postulantes omnes, etsi ex alumnis educatorii vel scholarum Instituti fuerint, per semestre probentur." [39]

It seems that before the publication of the 1901 *Normae* the postulancy could properly have been made in the house of the novitiate, but the postulants were, as far as possible, to be completely separated from the novices. "Non expedit ut postulantes cum novitiis convivant." [40]

The bishop of the diocese in which was located the house of the postulancy was not to concern himself, except in institutions of purely diocesan approval, with the admission to the postulancy properly so called, nor was his permission to be sought in order to receive a candidate who was desirous of entering the institute.[41]

2. *Papal Legislation*

The postulancy was required solely by special law until June 28, 1901, when the *Normae* of the Sacred Congregation of Bishops and Regulars brought the congregations of women religious within the direction and spirit, if not strictly under the obligation, of the common law. It must be remembered that this decree affected only institutes of women religious with simple vows, and it was expressly stated in the *Normae* themselves that numbers 64 and 65 pertained only to sisters. Nevertheless, Schaefer (1877-1948)[42] stated that it was the practice of the Sacred Congregation of Religious to extend these provisions to institutes of men religious also.

It is important to note here that the *Normae* were not laws; they served as directive provisions in the establishment of congregations

---

[39] S. C. Ep. et Reg., *Mexicana,* 22 maii 1896, ad 14 (Filiae Immaculatae Conceptionis)—Battandier, *loc. cit.*

[40] S. C. Ep. et Reg., 1 ian. 1862, ad 6um—Battandier, *loc. cit.*

[41] S. C. Ep. et Reg., 14 mart. 1841—Battandier, *ibid.,* p. 99.

[42] *De Religiosis ad Norman Codicis Iuris Canonici* (4.ed., Romae: Typis Polyglottis Vaticanis, 1947), n. 766 (hereafter cited *De Religiosis*).

whose members professed simple vows. They did not affect such congregations as were already in existence, nor did they bind under pain of invalidity, except when they repeated some invalidating requirement of the common law.

It is Chapter Four of the *Normae*, entitled *De Postulantibus*, which is of interest to the present discussion. In it, are contained the following requirements:

> 63. Ad admissionem postulantium requiritur et sufficit licentia moderatorum generalium, vel provincialium in suis provinciis (Cf. const. *Conditae*, part. II, n. 1).
>
> 64. Puellarum aspirantium probatio praevia, quae *postulatus* appellatur, congruentius fit in domo novitiatus, in loco tamen, si commode fieri potest, a novitiis separato. Sed annuente moderatrice generali vel provinciali, fieri aliquando potest in alia domo Instituti, dummodo in ea moretur notabilis sororum numerus, et disciplina iuxta Constitutiones religiose servetur, sub speciali cura alicuius probatae sororis.
>
> 65. Tempus *postulatus* non infra sex menses, nec ultra annum perduret. Moderatrix generalis, ex iusta causa, hoc tempus aliquanto prorogare poterit in casibus particularibus; sed prorogatio tres menses, non excedat.[43] (Writer's Italics).

The first thing, then, that the *Normae* decided with respect to the postulancy was to whom the right of admitting postulants belonged. In general, it can be said that in the legislation of the time the various acts whereby persons were admitted to the religious life were reserved to the superioress with her council. This, however, was not the case with the admission to the postulancy, which was considered simply the vestibule or the ante-chamber to the religious life. The postulancy did not put one under the same obligations as did one's admission to the religious life properly so called. The postulant did not have a proper religious habit; in fact, it was allowable for her to wear her secular clothes. If, in institutes of women religious, usage dictated that the young woman should receive a modest black habit, it was in virtue of such a reasonable

[43] *Normae Secundum Quas S. Congregatio Episcoporum et Regularium procedere solet in Approbandis Novis Institutis Votorum Simplicium* (Romae: Typis S.C. De Propaganda Fide, 1901). These *Normae* may be found in Schaefer, *De Religiosis*, pp. 1102-1135.

custom, and not by any precept of the constitutions, for to these the candidate was not officially subject. Hence admission to the postulancy, which was not the equivalent of an admission to the religious life properly so called, was reserved to the superioress general or to the provincial in her own province; it was not necessary for either of them to consult with their respective councils and to abide by their advice. The admission of postulants, therefore, was a direct exercise of the power of the superioress. The *Normae* in number 63 made this abundantly clear.

The major superioress, who had the right to admit persons to the postulancy without asking the consent of her council, could in similar fashion dismiss a postulant. This was clearly indicated in the *Normae*, in number 271, 7°, where the deliberative vote of the council was demanded only for the admission and the dismissal of the novices, and nothing was said of such a vote when the postulancy was spoken of. As a consequence, if the superioress saw that a candidate was not properly suited for the institute, either because of some physical defect or because of the absence of some necessary moral qualification, she could on her own authority dismiss the postulant and send her back to her family.

Of course, it goes without saying that the superioress did well if she kept in mind the adage, "*turpius eiicitur quam non admittitur hospes,*" and that consequently, before proceeding with any such dismissal, she at least sought the prudent advice and counsel of others.

The second point that the *Normae* regulated in regard to the postulancy was the place in which it should be made. The general rule was that the postulants should be gathered in the novitiate house, wherein they were, as far as it was possible, to have a section separate from that of the novices, and, *a fortiori*, from the professed religious. This prescription, however, was not so rigorous that the superioress general or the provincial could not permit the period of the postulancy to be spent in another house of the institute under the following conditions: a) that there were in that house a sufficient number of religious; b) that the regular observance was religiously maintained therein, and c) that the postulants were placed under the special care and direction of a religious of approved virtue.

The third and last point which the *Normae* treated concerning the postulancy was its duration. Any constitution drawn up after the issuance of the *Normae* had to fix a certain duration of time for the postulancy, which could vary between the two terms of six months and one year. Thus, for example, the constitutions could require a postulancy of six, seven, ten or twelve months, but not one of five or thirteen months. At the expiration of the duly allotted time, if the superioress felt that she was still not sufficiently well acquainted with the character of the candidate, it was permitted to her to prolong this time, in particular cases, for another three-month period, but not any longer. For such a prolongation the *Normae* in number 65 required a just cause, which could only be the state of uncertainty in which the superioress found herself at the close of the prescribed probationary period with respect to the suitability of the candidate for admission to the religious life.

This, then, between 1901 and 1918 was the pre-Code legislation for the regulation of the postulancy in institutes of women religious with simple vows whenever such institutes were formed or established.

Much of this legislation has become, since the advent of the present Code, the universal law for postulants.

CHAPTER III

POSTULANCY IMPROPERLY SO CALLED

Besides the canonical one, there exists also another postulancy which differs in a number of respects from its canonical counterpart. Among the chief differences between these two, the following may be enumerated:

a) This so called postulancy does not have a definite period of time determined by the law, but it includes the time spent in high schools (*gymnasia*), which varies, according to the customs of the various countries, from four to nine years.[1]

b) This postulancy exists generally in institutes of clerical religious, whose members are destined for the clerical state.

c) The purpose of this postulancy is the reaping and protecting of vocations, which, as sad experience teaches, is all too difficult unless it is done very early in the life of the prospective candidate. This same difficulty now exists both for the religious clergy of nearly every nation, as well as for the secular clergy. Hence the necessity of instituting religious seminaries after the example of those which serve for the training of secular priests.

d) Another purpose of this postulancy, which usually, but not necessarily, coincides with the first, is the observance of that wise directive, according to which the novitiate should not be begun until the curriculum of the gymnasium has been completed.[2] Hence for all those who seek admission to the novitiate, but have not yet made or completed these studies, religious schools have been instituted in which religious vocations are gathered, protected and cultivated.

---

[1] Cf. "Consultationes," *Apollinaris* (Romae, 1928—), VII (1934), 492-499.

[2] Cf. S.C. de Religiosis, declarationes, 7 sept. 1909, ad 5um—*AAS,* I (1909), 703; declar. 21 dec. 1909—*AAS,* II (1910), 35-36; Pius XI, ep. ap. *Unigenitus Dei Filius,* 19 mart. 1924—*AAS,* XVI (1924), 140.

e) For the beginning of this postulancy, or in other words, for entrance into religious schools of this sort, no specific age is required, as it is equivalently for the canonical postulancy; nor is the age requirement the same in all religious Orders or in all countries. It depends, among other things, on the time required for completing, according to the divers localities, the course of studies in the gymnasium.

Brief History of this "Postulancy"

Until the end of the eighteenth century there existed in the various religions Orders those adumbrations of the present-day canonical postulancy which have already been pointed out.[3] But this other postulancy in the broad sense of the term was completely unknown in these Orders, for no need had ever been felt for it. There had always been an abundance of mature and sufficiently prepared vocations.

It was in France, towards the end of the eighteenth century, that this postulancy made its first appearance. The occasion for its institution was the civil legislation of King Louis XV in March of the year 1768 concerning the reformation of the Orders of regulars. With this enactment he forbade anyone to make profession of vows before the age of twenty-one. In order, therefore, that the Orders might continue to receive candidates and train and educate them before their entrance into the novitiate, there was created this first probationary period, in which they were to be instructed in virtue and knowledge to an equal degree.[4]

In the older congregations of men there was frequently found that brief period of preparation immediately prior to the novitiate that existed in the Orders of monks and regulars.[5] This postulancy,

---

[3] Cf. *supra*, pp. 4-24.

[4] Cf. Commentaire sur la Règle de Saint Benoit per l'Abbé de Solesmes, p. 427—*Commentarium pro Religiosis* (Romae, 1920-1934: ab anno 1935, *Commentarium pro Religiosis et Missionariis*), XVI (1935), 149 (hereafter cited *CpR* and *CpRM* respectively).

[5] Cf. *supra*, pp. 38-41.

in the wide sense of the term, was a rather ancient institution in some of the lay congregations.[6]

In the clerical congregations, this postulancy, under the form of an Apostolic School, was not found, as far as is evident, before the second half of the last century.[7]

The greater part of the congregations of the later years of the nineteenth and of the early years of the twentieth century established such Apostolic Schools.

The non-canonical postulancy was generally unknown among congregations of women religious. Now, however, these too have frequently founded such institutions for the fostering of vocations and the education of their candidates.

These Apostolic Schools exist in a number of diverse forms, and more or less closely resemble the institute of the canonical postulancy. Although the Code does not speak of this postulancy in the broad sense, nevertheless, by analogy some of the laws, jurisprudence and doctrine concerning the canonical postulancy can be applied equally to this institute and in some instances should be so applied.

---

[6] Cf. *Règle de gouvernement de l'Institut des Frères des Ecoles Chretiénnes* (ed. 1923) Ch. II (III) Petit-Novitiat, n. 39—*CpRM,* XVI (1935), 150.

[7] Cf. George, *Le Très Révérend Père Achile Desurmont* (1924), 314 ff; Aguilar, *Historia de la Congregación* (ed. Barcelona 1901) I, 577 ff.—*CpRM,* XVI (1935), 151, nota 61.

PART II — CANONICAL COMMENTARY

CHAPTER IV

THE CONCEPT OF A CANONICAL POSTULANCY

A. The Nature of the Postulancy

Although the Code nowhere furnishes a definition of the postulancy, from its nature and puropse as there outlined and from its historical evolution one may define it as a time of preparation and probation during which, as preliminary to the novitiate, the person who seeks to enter religion lives as a qualified guest-student in the religious house, and follows the way of life of the members of that institute, under the vigilance of the religious superior. It should give the superiors an opportunity to observe the candidate, and the candidate an opportunity to become acquainted with the obligations of the religious life.[1]

In pre-Code law, as in the common law today, the postulancy was considered as the vestibule of the canonical novitiate, and bore a marked similarity to it. It was intended as a period of preliminary probation for those who were eventually to make profession of perpetual vows—especially for women religious and for those who were destined for a more humble condition of life, such as lay brothers. In the earlier days of monasticism its counterpart is discernible in the time required to be spent knocking at the door of the monastery and serving in the guest-house, as ordered in the Benedictine and the other ancient monastic Rules.[2]

The term 'postulancy' has not always been applied to this initial period of probation by the various religious institutes which required it by special law. In the past the postulancy was known

[1] Schaefer, *De Religiosis*, n. 764; Fanfani, *De Iure Religiosorum ad Normam Codicis Iuris Canonici* (3. ed., Rovigo: Istituto Padano de Arti-Grafiche, 1949), n. 188 (hereafter cited *De Iure Religiosorum*); Creusen, *Religious Men and Women in the Code* (4. Eng. ed., Milwaukee: Bruce, 1940), n. 171 (hereafter cited *Religious in the Code*).

[2] Cf. *supra*, pp. 7; 12; 15; 19.

as the little novitiate, the aspirantship, the first probation and the candidature.[3] The Code refers to those who have already entered religion and the postulancy as aspirants,[4] as candidates,[5] and as postulants.[6] Schaefer, however, mentioned that it is the practice of the Sacred Congregation of Religious in approving constitutions not to allow novices and postulants to be referred to as aspirants or candidates.[7] These terms are reserved for those who are seeking admission into religion before they actually enter upon their postulancy.[8]

Since, then, the postulancy is a period of trial and probation antecedent to the novitiate, it follows that admittance into the postulancy is by no means the same as entry into religion, but is described by commentators as placing one at the doors of religion or in the ante-chamber of the novitiate.[9] The present law of the novitiate concedes a certain incorporation into the community and the institute, as is evident from the fact that novices enjoy all the spiritual favors which are accorded to the professed religious, as well as certain other rights, but not all of these favors are granted to postulants, and hence the postulancy does not induce this incorporation.[10]

B. The Purpose of the Postulancy

The postulancy may be said to have a double purpose: one, when considered from the point of view of the candidate, and the other, when considered from the point of view of the superior. The postulancy should give the candidate an opportunity of becoming acquainted with the obligations of the religious life in general, and

[3] Schaefer, *De Religiosis*, n. 764.

[4] Canons 552, §2; 570, §2.

[5] Canon 2411.

[6] Canons 540, §2; 541.

[7] *De Religiosis*, n. 764.

[8] Larraona, "Commentarium Codicis," *CpRM*, XVI (1935), 145 nota 30.

[9] Cf. Schaefer, *loc. cit.*; *Larraona*, "Commentarium Codicis," *CpRM*, XVI (1935), 223.

[10] Coronata, *Institutiones Iuris Canonici ad Usum Utriusque Cleri et Scholarum* (5 vols., Vol. I, 4. ed., Taurini: Marietti, 1950), I, n. 566 (hereafter cited *Institutiones*).

with the rules, customs, and practices of the institute of his choice in particular. For the superiors it affords a time in which they may become acquainted with and try the aspirants or candidates, in order that those who give no hope of persevering or no signs of a religious vocation may be speedily eliminated. It also allows superiors to begin the instruction of the institute's future members in the rudiments of the spiritual and religious life, so that the novitiate which follows this period of preparation may be the more productive of good for the candidates.[11]

Hence the postulancy, by providing an adequate time of probation and preparation before recruits in religion are admitted to vows, acts as a safeguard for the stability of the religious state, and as a protection for the professed members of the institute as well as for the aspirants themselves.[12] It has always been the cherished desire of the Holy See, either explicitly or implicitly reflected in all its pre-Code documents on the postulancy and now in the Code itself, that by a lengthening of the period of time which one must spend in religion before one is allowed to make profession of vows the number of requests for dispensations from these vows should be greatly reduced.[13]

Since in the law's terminology postulants strictly do not come under the name either of religious or of novices,[14] they are not obliged to the regular religious observance. In view, however, of the end which the postulancy strives to attain, they must conform themselves to most of the practices of the professed members of the institute. This certainly appears to be the true mind of the legislator as deduced from pre-Code responses on this point[15] and

---

[11] Cf. Clemens VIII, const. *Cum ad regularem,* 19 mart. 1603—*Fontes* n. 189; Larraona, "Commentarium Codicis," *CpRM,* XVI (1935), 145; Schaefer, *De Religiosis,* n. 765; Creusen, *Religious in the Code,* n. 171.

[12] Cf. S.C. de Religiosis, decr. *Sacrosancta,* 1 ian. 1911—*Fontes,* n. 4407.

[13] Cf. preceding footnote; also S.C. de Religiosis, decr. *Quo propositum,* 15 aug. 1912—*Fontes,* n. 4412.

[14] Cf. canon 488, 7°; Larraona, "Commentarium Codicis," *CpRM,* XVI (1935), 224; Larraona, "Commentarium Codicis," *CpR,* IV (1923), 10.

[15] Cf., e.g., Response of the S. C. of Religious of May 29, 1913—*Del Boletin Oficial Eclesiástico de la Habana* de 30 julio de 1913, pp. 157-158.

from the text of the Code itself.[16] If the postulants were not expected to follow, and indeed quite exactly so, the acts of the community which pertain to the external religious discipline, then the requirement of the Code, namely that "the postulancy be spent in either the house of the novitiate or in another house of the institute in which the discipline prescribed by the constitutions is faithfully observed," would appear to be nugatory.

There is, in fact, little or no difference between the purpose of the postulancy and that of the novitiate. In the novitiate, however, the probation and testing are more exact and intense than in the postulancy, for the latter, as has been pointed out, serves simply as a previous probation.[17] While in essence the purpose of these probationary periods is the same, nevertheless, no one can deny that the postulancy in relation to the novitiate is in a much inferior position. Since admission to the latter is granted by a more solemn act, it is somewhat easier to depart or to be dismissed from the postulancy than from the novitiate.[18]

C. The Necessity of the Postulancy

Canon 539, § 1, which treats of the necessity of the postulancy, reads:

> *In religionibus a votis perpetuis mulieres omnes et, si agatur de religione virorum, conversi, antequam ad novitiatum admittantur, postulatum ad sex saltem integros menses peragant; in religionibus vero a votis temporariis, ad necessitatem et tempus postulatus quod attinet, standum constitutionibus.*

Under the present law all women religious ("*mulieres omnes*"), not only lay sisters and nuns, are required to spend a minimum of six months in the postulancy, provided that they are members of a religious institute of perpetual vows. It is of no importance, in so far as the postulancy is concerned, whether this institute is an

---

[16] Canon 540, § 1.

[17] Cf. *supra,* pp. 59-60; *Normae Secundum Quas Sacra Congregatio Episcoporum et Regularium procedere solet in Approbandis Novis Institutis Votorum Simplicium,* n. 64 (hereafter cited *Normae*).

[18] Schaefer, *De Religiosis,* n. 765.

order or a congregation, of papal or of diocesan approval. Both lay and choir religious are embraced within the scope of this canon.

If the institute is one of men religious who take perpetual vows, the law binds only the lay brothers (*"conversi"*) who are members of it.

Although Wernz-Vidal seemed to be of the opinion that the law of the postulancy applies also to teaching brothers,[19] the term *"conversi"* or lay brothers is commonly held as applying only to those who are engaged in manual labor or in domestic offices, and who enjoy no share in the government of the institute, since this is reserved to the "choir religious." [20] This interpretation seems to be the one which the Sacred Congregation has followed in approving constitutions since the Code.[21] Likewise, this interpretation is in accord with the principles contained in canons 18 and 6, 3°. It is true that the term *"conversi"* originally was used in designation of those who in adult life voluntarily renounced the world and entered religion, in order to distinguish them from the *oblati* or *nutriti*, who as children were offered by their parents to religion.[22] From the eleventh century, however, until the promulgation of

[19] *Ius Canonicum ad Codicis Normam Exactum* (7 toms. in 8 vols., Romae: apud Aedes Universitatis Gregorianae, Tom. III, *De Religiosis*, 1933), III, n. 242, nota (7) (hereafter cited *Ius Canonicum*).

[20] Vermeersch-Creusen, *Epitome Iuris Canonici cum Commentariis ad Scholas et ad Usum Privatum* (3 vols., Vol. I, 7. ed., Mechliniae-Romae: Dessain, 1949), I, n. 665 (hereafter cited *Epitome*); Fanfani, *De Iure Religiosorum*, n. 189; Schaefer, *De Religiosis*, n. 768; Larraona, "Commentarium Codicis," *CpRM*, XVI (1935), 152; Bastien, *Directoire Canonique a l'Usage des Congregations a Voeux Simples* (3. ed., Bruges: Beyaert, 1923), p. 51, note 2 (hereafter cited *Directoire Canonique*); Chelodi, *Ius Canonicum de Personis* (3. ed., curavit Pius Ciprotti, Vicenza: Libreria Moderna Editrice, 1942), p. 414, nota 4 (hereafter cited *Ius de Personis*); Coronata, *Institutiones*, I, n. 567, nota 5; Raus, *Institutiones Canonicae iuxta Novum Codicem Iuris pro Scholis vel ad usum Privatum Synthetice Redactae* (2. ed., Lugduni, Parisiis: Vitte, 1931), p. 298.

[21] Cf., e.g., *Constitutiones Ordinis Hospitalarii S. Joannis de Deo* (Romae, 1927), n. 41: "Postulatus tempus erit ad tres menses. Provincialis tamen iusta de causa hoc tempus prorogare poterit, sed non ultra adiud trimestre."

[22] Cf. *supra*, p. 26.

the Code this term was more properly employed in designation of that class of religious which was destined for manual labor, and occupied a secondary position especially in clerical religious Orders.[23] It became necessary, therefore, to distinguish between *conversi* and other male lay religious. Thus in a lay religious institute it was possible to have two distinct classes, the lay religious ("choir religious"), who carried on the work of the institute (teaching, nursing), and the *conversi*, who performed the manual and domestic tasks in the religious house.

The whole tenor of the decree *Sacrosancta*, issued by the Sacred Congregation of Religious on January 1, 1911,[24] made it abundantly clear that the pre-Code law of the postulancy was applicable only to the *conversi*, or the lay religious destined for the performance of the domestic offices.

Since, then, the term "*conversi*" for a period of roughly nine hundred years before the promulgation of the Code referred only to lay brothers properly so-called, it seems that this term as now used by the Code should retain this signification as its proper meaning.[25] And since the pre-Code common law in legislating for men religious of solemn vows ordered only the *conversi* or lay brothers to make a postulancy of two years, and this law was universally understood as binding only those religious who were properly engaged in domestic tasks, and since this legislation was in part re-enacted by the Code, this law must be interpreted in the light of the ancient law, in so far as the two are in agreement.[26] Now, both laws agree in this that only the *conversi* are mentioned, and therefore it seems safe to conclude that, until the Holy See shall authoritatively decide otherwise, male lay religious who are not lay brothers are not embraced in the scope of this requirement of canon 539, § 1.[27]

If in a certain lay religious institute there is only one class of lay religious, then the members of this institute are not *conversi*

---

[23] Schaefer, *De Religiosis*, n. 768; *supra*, pp. 26-29.

[24] *Fontes*, n. 4407.

[25] Cf. canon 18.

[26] Canon 6, 3°.

[27] Cf. *supra*, p. 63, note 20.

properly so called, and hence are not held to the common law postulancy. Only those religious are termed *conversi* who within the religious institute form a second class, whose main occupation is the domestic offices of the religious house, and which has no part in the government of the institute.[28] Likewise, if in certain religious institutes which consist of several classes of religious only one particular class is admitted to the profession of perpetual vows, then only for that class will the postulancy be of necessity by the common law.[29]

For those religious, even of perpetual vows, who aspire to the clerical state no postulancy is demanded by the Code. The reason for this seems to be the fact that future clerics are subjected to very thorough and special examinations as to their sacerdotal vocation, and hence the safeguard of the postulancy is for them not so necessary as it is for those whose formation and training are not so long and arduous.[30] Also excluded from the ambit of canon 539, § 1, are those men and women who belong to societies which prescribe a common life, but in which there is no profession of vows.[31]

It is quite clear from a reading of the canon under consideration that, if religious institutes lack perpetual vows, then they have no postulancy other than that which the constitutions may prescribe. This is true even for clerical religious institutes where members profess only temporary vows. Hence for such institutes (in which there is no profession of perpetual vows) the postulancy may or may not be required, since the law demands only compliance with the constitutions in this instance.

Vermeersch-Creusen make it clear that, if the religious insti-

---

[28] Schaefer, *De Religiosis*, n. 768; Larraona, "Commentarium Codicis," *CpR*, VIII (1927), 172 nota (413).

[29] Vermeersch-Creusen, *Epitome*, I, n. 665; Wernz-Vidal, *Ius Canonicum*, III, n. 242. Fanfani, however, (n. 189) held that in this case the institute must be considered one of perpetual vows, and hence both classes would be required to make a postulancy.

[30] Schaefer, *De Religiosis*, n. 768; Voltas, "Consultationes," *CpR*, II (1921), 220.

[31] Schaefer, *loc. cit.*; Larraona, "Commentarium Codicis," *CpRM*, XVI (1935), 152.

tutes lack perpetual vows, they have no postulancy other than that which the constitutions prescribe.[32] The vast majority of the constitutions of religious institutes of temporary vows, both of men and of women religious, require that some time be spent in a period of preliminary training prior to the novitiate. Generally such a postulancy enjoined by the constitutions will be shorter and milder than that of the common law.[33] Sometimes the whole matter is left to the prudence and determination of the superiors of the novitiate.[34]

The postulancy is not obligatory by common law on religious of temporary vows because such religious are not bound to the divine service by a wholly irrevocable bond. While their adequate training and probation are also a matter of grave concern to the Church, it is evident that even greater care must be exercised in the case of those who will profess perpetual vows. The postulancy imposed by the constitutions is equivalent to the canonical postulancy, and for religious without perpetual vows takes its place. It, too, as far as its juridical effects are concerned, must be considered as a true canonical postulancy.[35]

It may be helpful to consider at this point a practical problem in relation to the necessity of the postulancy as it is stated in the first paragraph of canon 539. Does the law of this canon apply in the case of a religious, for example, who has completed some months of training as a novice-cleric in an institute of perpetual vows, and then decides to become a lay brother in the same institute?

Goyeneche[36] definitely maintains, and Larraona seems to concur in the opinion,[37] that the postulancy for lay brothers (*conversi*) need not be fully complied with if the candidate has had some previous probation as a clerical novice in the same institute. If the

---

[32] *Epitome*, I, n. 665.

[33] Larraona, "Commentarium Codicis," *CpRM*, XVI (1935), 152.

[34] Cf., e.g., *Constitutions of the Oblates of Saint Francis de Sales* (Childs, Maryland, 1927), n. 9, p. 9.

[35] Larraona, "Commentarium Codicis," *CpRM*, XVI (1935), 225, V cum nota (75).

[36] "Consultationes," *CpRM*, XIX (1938), 14.

[37] "Commentarium Codicis," *CpRM*, XVI (1935), 153.

period of previous probation has exceeded the six months required by the Code, then the postulancy in this instance may be completely omitted.

While the writer is in perfect accord with this view, he realizes that there are strong arguments in favor of the observance of the postulancy for lay brothers in the case outlined above. The first of these is based on the wording of canon 539, § 1, which unconditionally states that lay brothers in an institution of perpetual vows must undergo a postulancy of at least six months. The superior is not as liberty to omit or even to shorten this requirement, regardless of what weighty reasons might be advanced, whether it be the sanctity, moral worth, or apt disposition of the aspirant, or his previous training even in one of the schools maintained by the institute. There is no mistake about the clarity of the common law; it presents a strong argument for the application of the law to the case under discussion.

This view, i.e., that the postulancy for lay brothers must in the above case be still undertaken in full, gains additional support from a consideration of canon 558. This canon states that in institutes wherein there are two classes of members, e.g., clerics and lay brothers, the novitiate made in preparation for membership in one class is not valid for membership in the other class. While it is true that this canon is treating of the novitiate proper and does not refer to the postulancy, it at least clearly indicates that the legislator is in favor of a separate training for the two classes. Hence this canon seems to support the contention that the postulancy for lay brothers must be undergone completely, even in the case of one who transfers from the class of clerical novices to that of the lay brothers after he has passed some months in the novitiate of the clerics. Thus such a one would be held to the law of the postulancy no matter how long a time he had already previously spent in the clerical novitiate.

Despite the two arguments presented above the writer still feels that the contrary opinion in favor of the omission or of the reduction of the postulancy in the instance given does not lack probability in view of the argumentation which follows. These arguments are based on canon 18, on the mind of the legislator in the present case as culled from a study of other canons, and on the consideration of the purpose of the postulancy itself.

In its legislation on the formalities and effects of the transfer of a religious to another institute the Code is quite precise. In canon 633, §1, wherein are stated the probationary requirements in such a transfer, the Code gives us the definite norm that the novitiate must always be repeated when a religious leaves his own institute and transfers to any other institute.[38] The common law states nothing else on the probationary requirements for a religious as a transferee. Only the repetition of the novitiate in the new institute is enjoined; absolutely no mention of the repetition of the postulancy is made. Since the Code is silent on the matter of a further probation, and since further to delay the profession of the religious who is involved in the transfer would be a restriction and a burden on him, it seems that there is warrant in this instance for a strict interpretation of the law.[39] Therefore, for a religious who transfers to another institute it is only the repetition of the novitiate that is required. Berutti appears to forbid absolutely the repetition of the postulancy upon the effected transfer of a religious.[40] Vermeersch-Creusen[41] and other authors concur in this opinion.[42] It seems, then, that one may safely regard canon 633 as an instance of an exception to the general norm on the necessity of a postulancy as that norm is contained in canon 539, § 1.

Since with reference to the transfer of a religious the Code does not make any distinction between the different institutes involved, be they Orders or congregations, be they of pontifical or of diocesan approval, or between the different classes of religious involved, that

---

[38] Canon 633, § 1: "Transiens ad aliam religionem novitiatum peragere debet." It is obvious that the subject refers to a *"religiosus,"* which is the word contained in canon 632, and that only a professed religious is indicated. This is certain from the whole context of canon 633.

[39] Canon 19.

[40] *Institutiones Iuris Canonici* (6 vols., Vol. III, *De Religiosis,* Taurini-Romae: Marietti, 1936), III, n. 145.

[41] *Epitome,* I, n. 792.

[42] Goyeneche, "De Transitu ad adiam Religionem," *CpR,* II (1921), 147; cf. also "Consultationes," *CpRM,* XIX (1938), 14; Coronata, *Institutiones,* I, n. 637, nota 4; Wernz-Vidal, *Ius Canonicum,* III, n. 420, II.

is, whether they be clerics or lay brothers, one may assume that no distinctions need to be made. Therefore, a religious of a certain institute, whether he be a cleric or a lay brother, is free to transfer to another class in the institute to which he is tranferring. Thus a professed cleric-religious may commence the novitiate for the lay brotherhood in the new institute.

The common law does not demand more than a repetition of the novitiate in the case of a religious who transfers to another institute, and this rule seems to apply by implication even to the case in which a cleric religious transfers to the lay brotherhood of another institute. It seems, then, that canonical equity demands that one must concede that no more than the novitiate is required when a professed religious transfers to another class *within the same institute*. Therefore the postulancy in this case may be omitted.

Canon 558 seems to contain this same conclusion, at least implicitly. This canon states that in institutes in which there are two classes of members, the novitiate made in preparation for one class (clerics) is not valid for membership in the other class (lay brothers). Here again we must notice the lack of any reference by the common law to the fact that the postulancy, too, would have to be repeated by a cleric-religious who wishes to become a lay brother within the same institute. Therefore, only the novitiate proper needs to be repeated; a repetition of the postulancy does not appear necessary.

If a clerical novice, when he has already completed several months of his probation in the novitiate, desires to transfer to the class of lay brothers in the same institute, the repetition of the entire novitiate for the lay brothers is an obligation which is certain. The obligation, however, to repeat the postulancy is at best only a doubtful one. In the absence, then, of any legislation on this point by the proper constitutions of that institute, canonical equity seems to require that the time which a cleric has already completed in his training should be combined with the several additional months needed for filling out a duration of six months for the postulancy, on the supposition, of course, that only a six-month postulancy is demanded and that the religious in question has not already spent the equivalent of this period in the clerical novitiate.

By this arrangement the requirements of canon 539, § 1, seem to be fulfilled in regard to those cases in which the religious transferee within the same institute has been in the clerical novitiate less than the minimum time of six months which is mentioned by the common law for the postulancy for lay brothers. If the novice in question has already passed more than six months in the clerical novitiate and then transfers to the lay brotherhood of the same institute, it seems that, in reliance upon the arguments presented above, he may be allowed to begin the lay brother's novitiate immediately. The postulancy in this case is supplied by the six months or more already spent in training in the clerical novitiate. This equivalent period of training in the novitiate appears to render a completely new postulancy useless.

A consideration of the end or purpose of the postulancy as an institute in law also seems to justify this conclusion. This period of preliminary probation was intended to furnish lay brothers and women religious with the advantage of a longer time in which to determine whether they were suited for the religious life, and thus to prevent the hasty assuming of its duties and obligations, and consequently to prevent defections from the ranks of religion. When one considers the case of a clerical novice transferring to the class of lay brothers within the same institute, canonical equity appears to demand that the time of training already undergone be considered sufficient for the initial acquaintance with the rule, constitutions and customs of the institute, which is the fundamental purpose of the postulancy. Is it not logical to suppose that one who has been a clerical novice will have a better appreciation for the dignity and worth of the religious life, and that such a person will in all probability be better able to make a judgment in regard to his embracing it, than one who has never aspired to be more than a lay brother? If one remembers that the postulancy was originally intended to be an aid for the accomplishment of these very requisites on the part of those whom the legislator judged to be less qualified to possess such appreciation and judgment, by reason namely of their sex or humble condition of life, the repetition of the postulancy in the case outlined above seems to be superfluous and at best only a doubtful obligation.

A case somewhat similar to the foregoing could arise if a religious sometime during the course of his novitiate left the religious state and then, repenting of his decision, returned to the religious house after only a brief absence from it. Must he repeat the postulancy? This case should be treated basically in the same way as the one discussed above. For canon 556, § 1, which specifically legislates on such interruptions of the novitiate, requires that the novitiate be recommenced and completed if the novice has left the house without the permission of the superior and with the intention of not returning. Here again the common law is silent on whether the postulancy also must be repeated. Since, however, this period of additional probation, i.e., the repeated postulancy, would carry with it for the religious, an odious connotation, a strict interpretation of this canon seems justified in accordance with the canonical principle, "*odia restringi, et favores convenit ampliari.*" [43] This opinion also seems in accord with the pre-Code common law, which did not always demand even a repetition of the novitiate in the case of a re-commencement of the religious life.[44]

Likewise in this case the principal purpose of the postulancy, namely, the furnishing of a period of preliminary investigation and training in the rules, constitutions, and customs of the institute, has already been achieved in consequence of the time spent in the first postulancy and the novitiate. Hence it seems useless to insist upon a repetition of the postulancy. In the absence of special leg-

---

[43] Reg. 15, R. J., in VI°

[44] Cf. Pirhing, *Ius Canonicum in Quinque Libros Decretalium Distributum* (Dilingae, 1722), Lib. III, tit. XXXI, n. 43; Schmalzgrueber, *Ius Ecclesiasticum Universum* (5 vols. in 12, Romae, 1843-1845), Lib. III, tit. XXXI, n. 70; S. C. C., *Neapolitana,* mense nov. 1605—Pallottini, *Collectio Omnium Conclusionum et Resolutionum quae in causis propositis apud Sacram Congregationem Cardinalium S. Concilii Tridentini Interpretum prodierunt ab eius institutione, anno MDLXXIX ad MDCCCLX, distinctis titulis alphabetico ordine per materias digestas* (18 vols., Romae, 1868-1893), Vol. XV, s.v. *Professio religiosa,* II, n. 31 (hereafter cited Pallottini); S. C. C., *Messanen.,* 1613 — Pallottini, *ibidem,* n. 38.

islation on this point by the constitutions of the institute, no certain obligation to repeat it may be said to exist.

This same solution may be applied to the case in which a religious is forced for some reason to interrupt his novitiate by an absence from the novitiate house beyond thirty days. The common law in canon 556, § 1, demands only that the novitiate proper be repeated, and may be held to allow, at least implicitly, the omission of the postulancy.

It must, however, be pointed out, both in the case under discussion and in the one of a religious returning to the house after he has abandoned it, that in the light of the older law and of canonical equity a repetition of the postulancy seems called for if the period of time spent in the world is so long that either the moral character of the novice, or the status of the institute, has in the meanwhile undergone a notable change.[45] It is true that the commentators prior to the Code spoke only of repeating the novitiate under such circumstances, for a common law postulancy did not yet exist. They regarded this reassumption of the religious life as identical with a completely new entry into religion. Therefore the writer feels confident in asserting that a repetition of the entire postulancy would be demanded today in all cases of this kind.

There is yet another instance in which it seems that the postulancy need not be made. The reasons for allowing the omission of the postulancy in this case are the same as the ones mentioned above, namely, the ruling of canon 18 and the consideration of the purpose of the postulancy. By canon 640, § 2, if a secularized religious, in virtue of an apostolic indult, is re-admitted into his religious institute, he must make a new novitiate, but the law has nothing to say in regard to the repetition of the postulancy. Hence, in line with the argumentation already presented, it appears safe to conclude that such a religious on being re-admitted to religion need not repeat his postulancy.[46]

The conclusion that there does not effectively exist any obligation to repeat the postulancy in the case of a transfer, or of an

[45] Pirhing, Lib. III, tit. XXXI, n. 43.

[46] Larraona, "Commentarium Codicis," *CpRM*, XVI (1935), 223.

interruption of the novitiate, or also of an interruption of religious profession, is drawn from the principles of canon 18, from the implications contained in related canons of the Code, from the purpose or end of the postulancy, and from the general principles of canonical equity. No attempt has been made to suggest a certain norm. But it appears useful here to recall that according to canon 15 a doubtful law does not beget certified obligations, and hence this canon is applicable to those cases in which the making or repeating of the postulancy is at best of doubtful obligation.

CHAPTER V

THE TEMPORAL REQUIREMENT IN THE CANONICAL POSTULANCY

A. The Duration of the Postulancy

The description of the time element of the postulancy as contained in the words of canon 539, § 1, "at least six months" ("*ad sex saltem integros menses*"), clearly indicates that the Code favors a half-year period as the *minimum* time to be spent in the postulancy by those for whom the postulancy is obligatory by common law.[1] The constitutions are at liberty to demand a longer or even a shorter period for all religious of communities wherein there is profession of only temporary vows, because this elasticity is expressly allowed in the canon under consideration. Some authors,[2] however, point out that the Commission on Religious Institutes greatly desired that the time duration of the postulancy be *definitely* stated in those constitutions which require a postulancy, and not be loosely indicated by such phrases as, e.g., "at least six months," or "at least six or nine months." Nevertheless, there are not wanting examples of particular constitutions which leave this period indefinite.[3]

Some authors are of the mind that the constitutions cannot prescribe a period of postulancy which is longer than one year. Biederlack (1845-1930)—Führich (1869-1934) maintained that the con-

[1] Schaefer, *De Religiosis,* n. 774; Larraona, "Commentarium Codicis, *CpRM,* XVI (1935), 224.

[2] Vermeersch-Creusen, *Epitome,* I, n. 666; Larraona, "Commentarium Codicis," *CpRM,* XVI (1935), 225, VI; Battandier, *Guide Canonique,* n. 125.

[3] *Rules and Constitutions of the Congregation of the Most Holy Cross and Passion of Our Lord Jesus Christ* (Union City, N. J.: The Sign Press, ca. 1931), n. 28; *Constitutions of the Society of Mary* (Dayton, Ohio, 1937), n. 324.

stitutions which prescribed a longer period needed to be corrected.[4] In the first edition of his work *De Iure Religiosorum*, which appeared in 1920, Fanfani (1876-1955) in n. 158 seemed to hold the same opinion, but in the second edition, in 1925, he abandoned his former position, and he did not assign any time limit to the period required by the constitutions. An opinion he continued to maintain in the third edition of his work which appeared in 1949.[5] Augustine (1872-1943) in both the 1919 and the 1938 editions of his *Commentary* believed that the constitutions which prescribed a longer term than a year for institutes of perpetual vows were devoid of legal force.[6] While Chelodi (1880-1922) was ready to concede that the constitutions may require a longer period of time, he added that this did not seem to be in accord with the mind of the law or the obvious demand of equity, which, he maintained, is violated whenever the postulancy is excessively prolonged.[7]

The very wording, however, of the common law itself indicates the better and common opinion in this matter.[8] Even when treating of religious institutes of perpetual vows, canon 539, § 1, does not definitely state the maximum amount of time which must be spent in the postulancy. For the words "at least six full months" (*"ad sex saltem integros menses"*) rather indicate the minimum requirement of the common law. If the expression "at least" is to have any meaning at all, it can only be understood as allowing full liberty to the constitutions of the various institutes of perpetual vows to call for a postulancy of longer duration. Therefore, without any special

---

[4] *De Religiosis* (Oeniponte: Rauch, 1919), n. 62.

[5] *De Iure Religiosorum*, n. 189.

[6] *A Commentary on the New Code of Canon Law* (8 vols., St. Louis: Herder, Vol. III, 1st ed., 1919, 5. ed., 1938), III (5. ed.), 203.

[7] *Ius de Personis*, n. 264, nota 6.

[8] Cappello, *Summa Iuris Canonici in Usum Scholarum Concinnata* (3 vols., Romae: apud Aedes Universitatis Gregorianae, Vol. II, 4. ed., 1945), II, n. 34, 2 (hereafter cited *Summa*); Coronata, *Institutiones*, I, n. 567; Schaefer, *Das Ordenrecht nach dem Codex Iuris Canonici* (Münster: Verlag der Aschendorffschen Verlagsbuchhandlung, 1923), p. 147; Battandier, *Guide Canonique*, n. 123; Blat, *Commentarium Textus Codicis Iuris Canonici* (5 vols. in 6, lib. II, pars II-III, *Ius de Religiosis*, 3. ed., Romae: apud "Angelicum," 1938), II, n. 288 (hereafter cited *Ius de Religiosis*).

permission of the Holy See, the constitutions of these institutes may require a postulancy which is longer than six months, but they do not have the power to shorten the time to less than this without apostolic sanction. This, however, is not the case with religious institutes of temporary vows. Their constitutions, as is lucidly evident from the first paragraph of canon 539, have complete freedom either to demand a postulancy which will last for more than six months, or one which will be less than this half-year period.[9]

In order that no confusion be engendered by this discussion it is proper to note here that the point involved is not the prolongation of the original period of the postulancy, on which the Code indeed legislates in the second paragraph of Canon 539, and which will be treated in due course. At present there is under discussion the problem of the permissible length of the postulancy itself as set down by general and special law, in abstraction of course from the power of the major superiors to prolong this term by adding still another period of six months.

By far the greater number of authors and canonists acknowledges for the constitutions the right to prescribe for the members a longer original period of postulancy than the six months which the Code mentions. The contrary opinion is, according to Cappello, manifestly in opposition to the Code, which does not exclude, but rather favors a longer period for the postulancy.[10] Larraona, Vermeersch-Creusen and Coronata[11] are unable to see how anyone could deduce either from the first or from the second paragraph of canon 539 any argument that would militate against the right inherent in the constitutions to extend the original term of the postulancy beyond the six months stated in the common law. In an early work[12] Schaefer (1877-1948) seemed to think that it was rightful for the constitutions also to shorten the term proper of the postulancy to less than six months, even as they could extend

[9] Schaefer, *De Religiosis*, n. 774.

[10] *Summa*, II, n. 34, 2.

[11] "Commentarium Codicis," *CpRM*, XVI (1935), 225; *Epitome*, I, n. 617; *Institutiones*, I, n. 567.

[12] *Das Ordensrecht*, p. 147.

it to more than a year. In a later work,[13] however, he amended his position by stating that the special permission of the Holy See would be required for the constitutions to shorten the postulancy to less than six months. This rule is applicable, of course, only to those for whom the postulancy is of obligation by common law, namely, to all women religious of perpetual vows and to the *conversi* in institutes of men religious with perpetual vows. Among many other authors who held the opinion that in constitutions there may be demanded a longer period for the postulancy than that stated in the common law, one may mention also Battandier (1850-1921)[14] and Blat (1870-1943).[15]

The Sacred Congregation of Religious on July 16, 1931, issued special regulations and prescriptions for the extern sisters in the cloistered communities of nuns. Among other things the Sacred Congregation ordered one full year of postulancy for all candidates before they should be clothed with the habit of the novices.[16] This decree serves as an indication that a period of postulancy which is longer than the six months set down in the Code is certainly not contrary to the mind of the Holy See. As Berutti[17] remarks, the desirable length of the postulancy seems to be measured in some degree by the sex of the postulant and partly also by the humbler estate of life which the aspirant intends to embrace.

At the conclusion of the International Congress of Mothers General which was held in Rome in September, 1952, for the Superioresses General of Institutes of Pontifical Approval, Father Larraona. Secretary of the Sacred Congregation of Religious, delivered an address in which he stated that the Congregation is ready to consider the advisability of changes in the constitutions on certain points. In this connection he mentioned in regard to the postulancy:

---

[13] *De Religiosis* (4. ed., 1947), n. 774.

[14] *Guide Canonique,* n. 123.

[15] *Ius de Religiosis,* II, n. 288.

[16] Cf. S.C. de Religiosis, *Statuta a sororibus externis monasteriorum* monialium cuiusque ordinis servanda, 16 iul. 1931, C. III, art. 21—*Apollinaris,* IV (1931), 348.

[17] *Institutiones,* III, n. 64.

> The Postulancy is obligatory for all women religious. It must last at least six months. If the constitutions prescribe a postulancy of one year, the six months' prolongation is still permissible. The maximum length of the postulancy is eighteen months. Rome does not want the decision as to the admission to be delayed too long, and this is the reason why the time limit is imposed.[18]

Evidently Father Larraona must have been speaking in this section of his address only of women religious with perpetual vows, for otherwise his statement would have proved contradictory to the Code. While Larraona's address was of a purely private character, it certainly seems to confirm the majority view that the duration of the postulancy may be extended beyond the necessary period of six months mentioned in the common law. It also seems that one may infer that Rome would be unwilling to approve any constitutions which ordained a postulancy whose original term lasted more than one year. Both Schaefer[19] and Battandier[20] had earlier made the observation that most generally no constitutions prescribe a postulancy whose duration exceeds the period of a full year.

By way of summary it may be said that a due specification of the duration of the postulancy in institutes of temporary vows is left entirely to the constitutions, which may require one which is either longer or shorter than six months. In institutes of perpetual vows, for the religious for whom the postulancy is of obligation by common law, the minimum term of the postulancy is six months. It is permissible in the constitutions, even apart from apostolic approval, to extend this period, but it is not permissible to shorten it without apostolic sanction. The present practice of the Congregation seems to indicate that the original term of the postulancy should not be in excess of one year, lest the admission of the candidate be delayed too long.

B. The Prolongation of the Postulancy

The second paragraph of canon 539, which treats of the prolongation of the postulancy, states:

---

[18] *The Canon Law Digest, Supplement through 1953,* at canon 502.

[19] *De Religiosis,* n. 774.

[20] *Guide Canonique,* p. 97.

Superior maior praescriptum postulatus tempus potest prorogare, non tamen ultra aliud semestre.

The power that is here given to the major superior must not be confused with the option inherent in the constitutions of religious institutes by the common law (canon 539, § 1), namely, of extending the original term of the postulancy beyond the minimum requirement of six months. As is evident from what has been said above, it is possible for the postulancy in an institute to be of a year's duration, even before all consideration of a prolongation in the strict sense of the word as used by canon 539, § 2. The prolongation treated of in this section of the canon may be made at the discretion of the major superior, but without special authorization from the Holy See it may not extend beyond the period of six months mentioned in the common law. The major superior spoken of here will be the provincial or one designated by the special law.

While it is conceivable that this prolongation might in a particular case be made at the request of the postulant, it is always left to the discretion of the proper major superior to determine the exact period of prorogation that may seem feasible. A just cause is sufficient to allow the proper superior to effect this prolongation.[21] This power entrusted to the major superior to prolong the period of the postulancy manifests the intention of the legislator to make the length of this probation to be elastic in its character.

The final phrase of canon 539, "but not beyond another six months" ("*non tamen ultra aliud semestre*"), has occasioned a certain amount of controversy and discussion among the authors. The point at issue is the meaning of the word "*aliud*" in relation to the rest of the canon. In the first edition of his work, Fanfani[22] thought of this six months' period as being the correlative of the first six months of the postulancy, and therefore held that the entire term of the postulancy could not be prolonged beyond a year. The authors and commentators who were previously mentioned as supporting the opinion that allowed a maximum postu-

[21] Berutti, *Institutiones,* III, n. 59.

[22] *De Iure Religiosorum,* n. 158.

lancy of only one year seemed to adopt this interpretation of "*aliud.*" [23]

The better and all but common opinion in this matter does not favor this interpretation of "*aliud.*" The authors maintain that, even if the constitutions should prescribe a postulancy which lasts one year, it is still within the power of the major superior to extend this period by another six months. Coronata states that undue insistence is not to be placed on the literal wording of the canon, "*aliud semestre.*" Though the Code contemplates the case in which the constitutions prescribe a postulancy of six months duration, it does not limit the addition of another six months to this instance alone.[24]

The writer is in perfect agreement with the conclusion reached by Coronata, but it seems that the latter resorted to a forced restrictive interpretation of the text of the law. Canon 539 sets up the general norms which govern the postulancy in religious institutes, and nowhere is the term of the postulancy restricted to a period of six months. When the canon mentions six months it does so only to state a minimum requirement ("*ad sex saltem integros menses*"), which may easily be extended. Hence there seems to be some little difficulty in accepting Coronata's opinion in so far as it regards "*aliud*" as a correlative of a particular period of six months, which he believes the Code has chosen as an example in this instance. While admitting, with Vermeersch-Creusen, that this interpretation of the text, taken literally, has some justification,[25] it appears that the context demands that one regard "*aliud semestre*" as a simple addition to the duration of the postulancy required by the common or the special law. Thus Vermeersch-Creusen come to the same extensive application of "*aliud semestre*" as Coronata, but in a much simpler and more satisfactory manner. For them the clause "*non tamen ultra aliud semestre*" must be considered as absolutely synonymous with "*non tamen ultra sex menses,*" in line with the obvious demands of the context. "*Aliud*"

---

[23] Cf. *supra*, p. 74.

[24] *Institutiones*, I, n. 567.

[25] *Epitome*, I, n. 666.

according to this opinion refers to the postulancy as prescribed by either the common or the special law, no matter how long the basic term of the postulancy may be. This view is substantially shared by most of the other canonists.[26]

Of course the constitutions are to be followed if they permit the major superior to prolong the postulancy for a greater length of time. The superior general cannot as a policy reserve to himself this power of prolonging the original term of the postulancy. But the constitutions may reserve it to him, or otherwise limit or even completely exclude it.[27] To prolong the duration of the postulancy the major superior generally does not need to seek the consultation or consent of his council or chapter. If a vote of the council is needed, it will generally not be more than merely consultative.[28] This too, however, must be left to the more accurate determination of the individual constitutions.

C. The Computation of the Time of the Postulancy

The rules for the computation of the time of the postulancy follow, for the most part, the prescriptions of the common law for the computation of the time of the novitiate.[29] In the time for the postulancy, however, less rigorous adherence to mathematical divisions is demanded than in computing the novitiate year. The tenor of all the canons as well as the view of the commentators indicates that this is the correct interpretation of the mind of the legislator. Certainly the strictness used in computing the time with regard to the postulancy must be commensurate with the stringency

[26] Goyeneche, *Iuris Canonici Summa Principia de Religiosis* (Romae: Tip. Pol. "Cuore di Maria," 1938), n. 43 (hereafter cited *De Religiosis*); Berutti, *Institutiones*, III, n. 65; Bastien, *Directoire Canonique*, n. 79; Cappello, *Summa*, II, n. 34,3; Creusen, *Religious in the Code*, n. 172; *Chelodi, Ius de Personis*, n. 264, nota (6); Larraona, "Consultationes," *CpR*, III (1922), 14-15; "Commentarium Codicis," *CpRM*, XVI (1935), 227.

[27] Schaefer, *De Religiosis*, n. 775.

[28] Cf., e.g., *Constitutiones Ordinis Recollectorum Sancti Augustini* (Romae, 1937), n. 37, 4º.

[29] Cf. Balzer, *The Computation of Time in a Canonical Novitiate*, pp. 96-99.

of the basic obligation of the postulancy itself. But after the promulgation of the Code, with the possible exception of particular constitutions, nowhere is the postulancy considered as anything more than *preceptive,* the total omission of which would in no way affect the validity of the subsequent novitiate and profession.[30] The word *"peragant,"* as used in canon 539, § 1, implies, according to Vermeersch (1858-1936)-Creusen, that the obligation is of precept only, and this is the common opinion.[31] Wernz (1842-1914)—Vidal (1867-1938) called attention to the fact that, if the law does not state expressly or equivalently that the act is null and void, then according to canon 11 the prerequisite condition in question is not invalidating. This view receives confirmation, they maintained, in that the postulancy is not demanded in all religious institutes.[32] Unless the constitutions so prescribe, institutes of women religious, if they do not profess perpetual vows, are not bound to the observance of a postulancy.[33]

It is evident to all that the postulancy in contrast to the novitiate is of secondary importance. Accordingly the computation of the time spent in the former will be less rigorous than that of the time spent in the latter. No one, however, should conclude from this that the postulancy is not a matter of serious obligation. If any superior were to disregard the norms of the common law regarding the fulfillment of the prescribed time, he could be guilty of serious fault.[34]

According to Coronata, the period of the postulancy must be computed according to the principle given in canon 34, § 3, 3°.[35]

---

[30] Coronata, *Institutiones,* I, 567; Cappello, *Summa,* II, n. 34, 7; Wernz-Vidal, *Ius Canonicum,* III, n. 244; Berutti, *Institutiones,* III, n. 65; Canons 539, § 1; 11; Cocchi, *Commentarium in Codicem Iuris Canonici ad Usum Scholarum* (5 vols. in 8, Liber II, Pars II, *De Religiosis* (4. ed., Taurinorum Augustae: Marietti, 1946), II, n. 62 (hereafter cited *De Religiosis*).

[31] *Epitome,* I, n. 665; also the authors cited in the preceding footnote.

[32] *Ius Canonicum,* III, n. 244.

[33] Vermeersch-Creusen, *Epitome,* I, n. 665.

[34] Creusen, *Religious in the Code,* n. 177; Balzer, *The Computation of Time in a Canonical Novitiate,* p. 97.

[35] *Institutiones,* I, n. 567 c).

Many other commentators concur in this view.[36] This is the same norm that is used in the computation of the year of the novitiate.[37] There is no longer any doubt in regard to the application of this canon (34, §3, 3°) to the period of the novitiate since the official response of the Pontifical Commission for the Interpretation of the Code, dated November 12, 1922.[38] In view of the marked similarity of the period of the postulancy to that of the novitiate, the same norm of computation should be applied to both.

The employment of canon 34, §3, 3°, implies the use of the so-called *civil reckoning.* This form of reckoning is also known as the reckoning from day to day in opposition to the natural reckoning of time, which is designated as the reckoning from a given moment to a given moment, or from a precise hour to a precise hour. The civil reckoning deals with a period of time which for its beginning and end is determined from the very moment of the inception of the natural day, i.e., from midnight, and not from any hour of the day, as with the natural reckoning. The clearest and easiest way to distinguish the natural from the civil reckoning is to bear in mind that they are adequately specified by the assumption of diverse starting points. If no definite starting point or *terminus a quo* is assigned either by the occurrence of some fact or by some disposition of the law, the natural reckoning is to be followed. On the other hand, if a starting point is explicitly or even implicitly assigned by law or in fact, the civil reckoning is to be employed.[39]

That the novitiate year has such a starting point is not difficult to see, since canon 553 makes it clear that this is signalized in the reception of the habit, or in some other similar external sign or

---

[36] Schaefer, *De Religiosis,* n. 774, nota 55; Fanfani, *De Iure Religiosorum,* n. 189; Pejška, *Ius Canonicum Religiosorum* (3. ed., Friburgi Brisgoviae: Herder, 1927), p. 87; Cappello, *Summa,* II, n. 34, 2. Larraona, on the contrary, maintains that the norm to be used is the one that is stated in canon 34, § 2—*CpRM,* XVI (1935), 224. Cf. also Blat, *Ius de Religiosis,* II, n. 288.

[37] Balzer, *The Computation of Time in a Canonical Novitiate,* p. 123.

[38] *AAS,* XIV (1922), 661.

[39] Balzer, *The Computation of Time in a Canonical Novitiate,* pp. 136 ff.

ceremony prescribed by the constitutions as marking the starting point of the novitiate year.[40] This is an explicit determination of the starting point.

While the exact point of beginning of the postulancy is not so clearly indicated, canon 540, §2, seems to enact a provision which runs parallel to that of canon 553, insofar as the indication of the beginning of the postulancy is concerned. Canon 540, § 2, directs that the one entering the postulancy shall wear a plain garb distinct from that of the novices. Obviously this distinctive vesture, of whatever kind it may be, is assumed as the very outset of the postulancy. Its assumption may with good reason be argued as analogous to the reception of the habit mentioned in canon 553, or as implying an assignment of the starting point for the postulancy. As Balzer (1914-1947) pointed out,[41] the fact that canon 540 itself suggests this comparison with canon 553 by making mention that the habit of the postulants should be different from that of the novices seems to have been overlooked by the authors. They usually hold that the postulancy commences at the moment the candidate actually takes up residence as a postulant in the religious house, with the mutual consent of the superior and the candidate.[42] Even if one does not concur with the opinion which holds that the taking of some form of distinctive garb marks the inception of the postulancy, and even if the constitutions do not demand a more definite manner of marking this starting point, it seems that the taking up of residence as a postulant in the religious house may still be regarded as an implicit assignment of the starting point of the postulancy. Hence, whether one maintains that the postulancy begins with the taking of a habit, or in a manner determined by the constitutions, or by taking up residence in the house, the norm

[40] Canon 553: "Novitiatus incipit susceptione habitus, vel alio modo in constitutionibus praescripto." This implies, of course, the approval of the superior.

[41] *The Computation of Time in a Canonical Novitiate*, pp. 98-99.

[42] Vermeersch-Creusen, *Epitome*, I, n. 667; Wernz-Vidal, *Ius Canonicum*, III, n. 242; Coronata, *Institutiones*, I, n. 567, where he says that the Code does not demand any special formality.

for the computation of the time of the postulancy is that of canon 34, §3, 3°.

With the use of the civil reckoning, according to canon 34, §3, 3°, the time of the postulancy is so computed that the first partial day of this period is not counted, and the required time expires six months or more later on the completion of the final day which is dated with the same number. One does not count the first day because, in line with the civil reckoning, whenever the *terminus a quo* or the beginning of the period of time in question, by some act of formality recognized by law, does not coincide with the very beginning of the natural day, the rest of the first day is disregarded. The legal computation of the time of the postulancy, then, begins only after *midnight* of the first partial day spent by the candidate within the religious house as a postulant.

The period of the postulancy ends according to the same norm with the completion of the very last day bearing the same date, i.e., at the end of the same day of the month, six or more months later, on which the period had its beginning. For example, if a candidate were to begin his postulancy at 10 o'clock in the morning on the 25 of March, the actual legal or civil computation of the time would begin only at midnight of the first partial day spent in the religious house as a postulant, that is to say, it would begin at midnight of March 25-26. On the supposition that the postulancy in this case is of a six months' duration, it would end on the 25 of September, but only at the very last moment of this day, i.e., at midnight of September 25-26. If the superiors should desire that the postulant enter upon his novitiate immediately, he could not do so until after midnight of September 25-26, i.e., until sometime the next day, September 26.[43]

D. Interruptions of the Postulancy

Most authors are in agreement that according to the common law the time which one spends in the postulancy need not be continuous, for the Code states that the postulancy must last for at least six complete months ("*ad sex saltem integros menses*"),

---

[43] Balzer, *The Computation of Time in a Canonical Novitiate,* p. 99.

whereas in its advertence to the novitiate it orders that an entire and uninterrupted year be spent therein (*"per annum integrum et continuum"*).[44] Hence commentators allow minor interruptions, and require only a moral continuity, for the postulancy would defeat its purpose if it were broken up into several periods of time, each widely separated from the other.[45] For example, Wernz-Vidal said that the vigor of the law with regard to the continuity of the year of the novitiate should not be extended to the postulancy, and therefore the time of the postulancy need not be reckoned continuously, except in so far as it is necessary for a moral continuity. Hence a brief absence of fifteen days from the postulancy would not interrupt it, granted that the postulancy in this case is one of at least six months' duration.[46]

Since in the case of the novitiate the common law allows an absence of fifteen days with no obligation to supply them, the authors usually consider a similar absence as certainly not interrupting the postulancy, and as not needing to be supplied. They base their reasoning on the fact that the law of the novitiate imposes more strenuous and rigorous obligations that does that of the postulancy.[47] Since, however, the postulancy is normally a shorter period of time than the year of the novitiate, a proportionately shorter absence is therefore required in order to interrupt the moral continuity of the time of the postulancy. It seems that in the absence of more accurate legislation, one may safely take the opinion of Berutti as providing a serviceable norm. If the moral continuity of the postulancy is broken, even with the permission of the superior and for a just and reasonable cause, then he maintains that the postulancy must be begun anew. An absence of thirty days or

---

[44] Cf. canons 539, § 1, and 555, § 1, 2°.

[45] Vermeersch-Creusen, *Epitome,* I, n. 666; Schaefer, *De Religiosis,* n. 774; Coronata, *Institutiones,* I, n. 567; Berutti, *Institutiones,* III, n. 65; Chelodi, *Ius de Personis,* n. 264, nota (5); Cocchi, *De Religiosis,* n. 62. Larraona seems to maintain that the months of the postulancy must as a general rule be continuous.—"Commentarium Codicis," *CpRM,* XVI (1935), 224.

[46] *Ius Canonicum,* III, n. 242.

[47] Schaefer, *De Religiosis,* n. 774; Canons 556 and 572, § 1, 3°.

longer would certainly break the moral continuity, even if the initial term of the postulancy is more than six months. If the postulant is absent from the religious house for a period of time not beyond a duration of twenty days, then Berutti holds that the days need not be supplied.[48]

The writer admits that this opinion is a little broader than that of most authors, who rely on the norm of canon 556, § 2, which lays down the rule in regard to the novitiate, and imply that in the case of any absence of more than fifteen days from the postulancy it is required that the missing days be supplied. Nevertheless, the writer favors this opinion because of the greater freedom and lack of rigor found in the Code in regard to the postulancy in the matter of computation of the time.

Schaefer and Vermeersch-Creusen concur with the foregoing line of argumentation, provided the postulant, while he is absent from the religious house for fifteen days or less with the permission of the superior, perseveres in his intention of returning and continuing the postulancy. They propose also the case of a postulant who actually abandons the religious house with the intention of severing all connections with the religious institute, and they conclude that if the postulant has been away from the house for no more than fifteen days, the postulancy need not be recommenced from the very beginning. The time required for the period of the postulancy may accordingly be made up of a combination of all the days spent in the postulancy before and after the departure of the postulant from the religious house.[49] The entire relaxed and rather easy going tenor of the whole legislation in regard to the postulancy allows this departure from the stricter norm governing the novitiate which is contained in canon 556, § 1, and which demands that the novitiate must be recommenced and completed if the novice has left the house without the permission of the superior and with the intention not to return.

The teaching presented above also allows the superior the liberty

---

[48] *Institutiones,* III, n. 65.

[49] Schaefer, *Re Religiosis,* n. 774; Vermeersch-Creusen, *Epitome,* I, n. 666.

to shorten the postulancy by a few days whenever a just and reasonable cause exists. According to Coronata[50] there is absolutely no reason to deny the superior this prerogative. Many authors do not discuss this precise question, probably because they felt it to be superfluous in view of the generous norms allowed in the computation of the missing days of the postulancy. If, then, a truly just cause exists, as Creusen says,[51] it appears reasonable to assume that the superior may shorten the period of the postulancy by a few days. A just cause would exist, for example, when it is desirable that all the postulants be received into the novitiate in one group and when this would at the same time be impossible unless the postulancy for one or the other were shortened. The superior to whom this prerogative is granted is obviously the major superior, who has the power both to admit the postulants and to prolong the period of their postulancy. Schaefer and Fanfani likewise grant that the superior may for a just cause shorten the postulancy by a few days.[52]

[50] *Institutiones,* I, n. 567.
[51] *Religious in the Code,* n. 172.
[52] *De Religiosis,* n. 774; *De Iure Religiosorum,* n. 189, Dubium II.

CHAPTER VI

THE LOCAL REQUIREMENT IN THE CANONICAL POSTULANCY

A. The Place of the Postulancy

Canon 540, § 1, states the common law requirement for the place of the postulancy:

> *Postulatus peragi debet vel in domo novitiatus vel in alia religionis domo in qua disciplina secundum constitutiones accurate servetur sub speciali cura probati religiosi.*

As is evident from a reading of this canon, the Code does not impose any obligation of housing the postulants in the novitiate, nor does it even seem to suggest that it might be better that the postulancy be fulfilled in the house of the novitiate. An option is given for the selection of the novitiate house or of some other house of the institute.[1] In fact, Larraona points out[2] that if the constitutions of any institute renounce this option and speak either directly or indirectly of the necessity of spending the postulancy in the novitiate house, this section, according to the present practice of the Sacred Congregation of Religious, is expunged.

The choice between the house of the novitiate and any other suitable house as a place for the postulancy is left completely to the judgment of the major superior, who is at liberty to decide as he deems best. This legislation marks a change from the pre-Code *Normae*, which prescribed the novitiate as the most appropriate site of the postulancy, and allowed the general or provincial superior *per modum actus* to designate some other house for this purpose.[3]

---

[1] Schaefer, *De Religiosis,* n. 776; Larraona, "Commentarium Codicis," *CpRM,* XVI (1935), 308.

[2] "Commentarium Codicis," *loc. cit.*

[3] *Normae,* n. 64.

Certainly in view of canon 554, § 3, which orders superiors to assign to the novitiate house and to the house of study only such religious who are exemplary in their zeal for the observance of good discipline, the superior would indeed do well to designate one of these houses for the residence of the postulants. As has been pointed out, however, he is not constrained to do so; he may choose any other house of the institute in which the discipline prescribed by the constitutions is faithfully observed. It will usually happen that the choice will fall at least upon one of the fully integrated (*formatae*) houses of the institute, for the reason that in such a house it is easier to have this faithful observance of the constitutions.[4] This canon does not forbid the distribution of the postulants in many houses of the institute, nor the repeated transfer of a postulant from one house to another.[5] Experience, however, demonstrates that it is generally preferable for the postulancy to be made in the novitiate house. It can be taken as a thoroughly sound and general principle that the effect on postulants of separation from the master of novices is little instruction or formation in the religious life.

The Sacred Congregation of Bishops and Regulars several times condemned the practice of sending postulants to a house in which discipline was not perfectly carried out;[6] but even if these admonitions were not observed, that fact did not in any way affect the validity of the postulancy.[7]

B. The Separation of the Postulants

Although the Code contains no express prohibition that bars postulants from communing with the novices, it may be questioned whether they are forbidden to mingle with them in virtue of canon 564, § 1. The law mentions explicitly only that the novices

[4] Schaefer, *De Religiosis*, n. 776.

[5] Goyeneche, *De Religiosis*, p. 79, nota (16); Larraona, "Commentarium Codicis," *CpRM*, XVI (1935), 309.

[6] S.C. Ep. et Reg., 23 mart. 1860, 6 iun. 1860, 11 iul. 1860—Bizzarri, *Collectanea in Usum Secretariae Sacrae Congregationis Episcoporum et Regularium* (2. ed., Romae, 1885), 778, 781, 785 (hereafter cited Bizzarri).

[7] Coronata, *Institutiones*, I, n. 568.

must be separated from the professed religious. Its meaning, however, seems to be that externs as well are to be barred from communing with them.[8]

What, then, about the postulants? A response of the Sacred Congregation of Bishops and Regulars of January 1, 1862, as cited by Battandier, forbade postulants to live in the novitiate with the novices.[9] The *Normae*, on the contrary, permitted the postulants to live in the novitiate, but in a place apart from the novices, if this could be done.[10] This ruling, however, was not contained in the decree of the Sacred Congregation of Religious which first established the postulancy an an institute of the common law;[11] nor was it contained in a subsequent decree on the postulancy issued by the same Congregation in the following year.[12] The Code in canon 540, § 1, permits the postulants to live in the novitiate, but is silent on whether they may commune with the novices.

Although the commentators admit this, they nevertheless maintain that it is more in conformity with the spirit of the law that the novices be kept apart from the postulants. At least, so these canonists say, the lay postulants who may live with the lay novices should be separated from the choir novices and postulants.[13] It is the practice of the Commission for the Approbation and Revision of Constitutions, so Goyeneche points out, to support this view.[14] Yet in some religious institutes the postulants about to enter the novitiate usually live not only in the novitiate house, but also in the novitiate itself with the novices.[15]

---

8 Larraona, "Commentarium Codicis," *CpRM,* XXIV (1943), 203.

9 S. C. Ep. et Reg., 1 ian. 1862, ad 6um—Battandier, *Guide Canonique,* p. 97.

10 *Normae,* n. 64.

11 S. C. de Religiosis, decr. 1 ian. 1911—*AAS,* III (1911), 29-36.

12 S. C. de Religiosis, decr. 15 aug. 1912, nn. 2, 3—*AAS,* IV (1912), 565-566.

13 Canon 564, § 2; Schaefer, *De Religiosis,* n. 776; Goyeneche, "Consultatio," *CpR* XIV (1933), 356; Larraona, "Commentarium Codicis," *CpRM,* XVI (1935), 308-309.

14 "Art. cit.", *loc. cit.*

15 Larraona, "Commentarium Codicis," *CpRM,* XXIV (1943), 203, nota 1158.

The proper conclusion of this discussion, so it seems, is that, although communication and association between novices and postulants does not appear to be forbidden by the Code, nevertheless, if the constitutions or customary practice of an institute require that these two groups be separated, this requisite must be followed as a special law.

C. The Prefect of the Postulants

Regardless of what houses of the institute are designated as the residences for the postulants, canon 540, § 1, orders that the time of the postulancy must be spent under the special direction of an experienced religious. Number 64 of the *Normae* laid down the requirement that the postulancy be spent under the special care and direction of a religious of approved virtue (*"sub speciali cura alicuius probatae sororis"*). The decree *Sacrosancta Dei Ecclesia,*[16] to which canon 540, § 1, refers as its source, prescribed that a father, recommended by the maturity of his years and the manner of his life, be placed over the postulants for the purpose of insuring that from the very beginning the religious spirit and that of the order pervade their whole soul.[17]

This experienced religious, who has been designated by such titles as Prefect, Master, or Provost, even when the postulancy is located in the novitiate house, may be someone other than the master of novices. It generally will not be prudent, however, when the postulants are allowed to associate and commune with the novices, to have this division of authority. Such an arrangement could easily do harm to the unity of regime so necessary in the novitiate, and thus became manifestly opposed to canon 561, § 1.[18]

A workable arrangement in this situation would be the entrusting of the direction of the postulants to the *socius* of the master of novices, if there is one, or the appointing of the prefect of the postulants to serve also in this capacity. Thus unity of direction in the novitiate would be assured. But whenever this office does

[16] *Fontes,* n. 4407; *AAS,* III (1911), 29-36.

[17] Cf. *supra,* p. 35.

[18] Larraona, "Commentarium Codicis," *CpRM,* XVI (1935), 309.

not fall to the master of novices or his *socius* in the novitiate house, and whenever the postulants live outside this house, the appointment of some other religious is of obligation.[19] It appears that, if the constitutions contain nothing about the appointment of this official, then it pertains to the major superior (provincial) to determine who this prefect shall be.[20]

The common law does not set down any requirements for this experienced religious. It is sufficient, then, if he is a professed member of the institute and is possessed of approved virtue. In the constitutions there may, of course, be demanded other qualities more or less similar to those demanded by canon 588, § 2, of the master of the spirit, who is placed over the professed students in houses of study. Hence, it may be required that he be distinguished for prudence, charity, piety, and the faithful observance of the rule. Schaefer added that, when there is question of a clerical religious institute, then the postulants must be placed under the care and guidance of a priest.[21]

---

[19] Canon 540, § 1.

[20] O'Brien *The Provincial Superior in Religious Orders of Men,* The Catholic University of America Canon Law Studies, n. 258 (Washington, D. C.: The Catholic University of America Press, 1947), p. 85.

[21] *De Religiosis,* n. 776.

CHAPTER VII

OTHER REQUIREMENTS IN THE CANONICAL POSTULANCY

A. The Clothing of the Postulant

It is the second paragraph of canon 540 which gives us the scanty legislation of the common law in regard to the clothing of the postulants. It states:

> *Postulantes vestem induant modestam ac diversam a veste novitiorum.*

This regulation of the Code can be traced to the decree *Quo propositum* of the 15 of August, 1912,[1] in which in n. 3 it was ordained that those who were admitted to the postulancy should wear a garb of modest color which was to be different from the habit of the order (*"Postulantes admissae, utantur veste modesti coloris, diversa ab habitu Ordinis . . ."*). The Code now prescribes nothing more than that the vesture of the postulants be modest in every respect, and not the same as that worn by the novices. Most of the authors are of the opinion that this enactment of the common law does not require the postulants to be clothed with a distinctive garment, so that they may even spend this time in their secular dress.[2] Prümmer (1866-1931) stated[3] that, since the postulants can easily leave the postulancy, it is preferable that they wear only their secular garb throughout this period. The commentators do not even require that the postulants be clothed in a uniform manner, but they

---

[1] *Fontes*, n. 1412.

[2] Schaefer, *De Religiosis*, n. 773; Larraona, "Commentarium Codicis," *CpRM*, XVI (1935), 310; Beste, *Introductio in Codicem*, at canon 540, § 2; Coronata, *Institutiones*, I, n. 568, 2°; Creusen, *Religious in the Code*, p. 131, 2; Wernz-Vidal, *Ius Canonicum*, n. 243.

[3] *Manuale Iuris Canonici in Usum Scholarum* (5. ed., Friburgi Brisgoviae: Herder, 1927), p. 270.

add that nothing in the law bars the wearing of a distinctive religious garb during the term of the postulancy.[4] It is necessary, as Berutti points out,[5] that it be externally apparent that the postulants have not been received into the novitiate. Hence if they do wear a distinctive garb when it is so ordered by the constitutions, it must be different from the habit of the novices, which is assumed only at the beginning of the novitiate proper.[6] It is this act, if nothing else is indicated in the constitutions, that marks the inception of the novitiate.

It seems, then, to be the general opinion among canonists, when the constitutions are silent on this point, that the postulants should be clothed in such a manner that neither the material, nor the fashion, nor even the color of their garb smack of worldly vanity.

Despite this weight of authority, there are a few authors who seem to maintain that postulants should be granted a distinctive religious garb at the very outset of their postulancy.[7] Balzer[8] further added that, by analogy with canon 553, the act of receiving this habit should mark the canonical commencement of the postulancy. It is canon 540, § 2, itself which suggests this comparison with canon 553 by mentioning the fact that the vesture of the postulants should be different from that of the novices. Canon 570, § 1, also mentions the religious habit in connection with the postulancy. It certainly seems lawful, therefore, for an institute to require that its postulants be clothed with a distinctive religious garb. Moreover, for the reasons mentioned the present writer feels compelled to maintain that a distinctive uniform for postulants is a matter of obligation. In adopting this view the writer is fully aware that it is shared by only a minority of authors, yet it is this opinion which seems to be the more probable from intrinsic arguments. Neither this opinion, however, nor the majority view

---

[4] Cf. authors cited in footnote 2.

[5] *Institutiones,* III, n. 66, III.

[6] Canon 553.

[7] Balzer, *The Computation of Time in a Canonical Novitiate,* pp. 98-99; Fanfani, *De Iure Religiosorum,* n. 190; E; Pejška, *Ius Canonicum Religiosorum,* p. 87.

[8] *Loc. cit.*

expressed above is certain, and the latter has in its favor the weight of competent authority. Hence the principles of canon 15 will not allow one to maintain that there is a certified obligation to grant to postulants at the beginning of their postulancy a distinctive religious garb.

Of course, the guiding norm in this question as well as in others dealing in particular with the religious life must be the explicit provisions of the constitutions. If they do not contain anything more definite than does the common law, superiors may safely allow the postulants to spend the entire period of their postulancy in their secular garb, provided only that it be modest.

It appears, however, to be the practice of a number of institutes, particularly of women religious, to require that their postulants be clothed with a modified form of the religious habit, or in some other distinctive manner.[9]

B. The Law of the Cloister in Regard to Postulants: Penalties

Paragraph three of canon 540 legislates for the cloister of nun-postulants. It states:

> *In monasteriis monialium adspirantes, dum postulatum peragunt, lege clausurae tenentur.*

As is evident, this provision of the common law binds only the postulants in orders of nuns properly so called. They are bound by this law regardless of whether the monastery to which they belong is subject to the major or to the minor papal cloister. Nuns who are subject to the major papal cloister are those who lead the purely contemplative life and either actually take solemn vows or should take them according to their institute, but who because of a temporary exception take only simple vows. Likewise to be considered as nuns subject to the major papal cloister are those

[9] Cf., e.g., *Constitutions of the Missionary Servants of the Most Blessed Trinity* (Philadelphia, 1933), Chapter III, 9; *Constitutions of the Congregation of the Sisters of Notre Dame* (1937), Chapter V; *Constitutiones Ordinis Recollectorum Sancti Augustini,* n. 218.

who belong to a monastery in which they regularly lead a purely contemplative life, even though the Apostolic See, for serious reasons and as long as these reasons persist, may have imposed upon them or permitted to them the exercise of some works of the apostolate. In this case, however, only a few nuns and only a small part of the monastery, clearly distinct and separate from the part in which the community resides and follows the common life, may be destined for such works. Nuns who are subject to the minor papal cloister are those who belong to a monastery of solemn or simple vows in which many nuns and a notable part of the house are habitually destined for works of the apostolate.[10] Women religious other than those enumerated above as nuns who must observe either the major or the minor papal cloister are not bound by this regulation of the common law.[11]

Before the issuance of the decree *Quo propositum*[12] it was the general rule that postulants could not be received within the confines of the cloister of nuns without the previous permission of the Holy See. This decree, however, allowed postulants to be received into the cloister without this apostolic permission. Now it is required that postulants in orders of nuns have the permission of the local ordinary to enter the cloister.[13]

The decree *Quo propositum* had given rise to the question whether nun-postulants were to be subject to the same laws that bound nuns in the matter of departing from the cloister. To this question the Sacred Congregation of Religious replied that the nun-postulants could not leave the cloister unless they had a special indult of the Holy See.[14] It is this response that is cited in the footnote of the Code as the source of paragraph 3 of canon 540.

---

[10] See the general statutes appended to the Apostolic Constitution *Sponsa Christi*, 21 nov. 1950, Art. IV, § 2, 2°; § 3, 3°—*AAS*, XLIII (1951), 16-17; Instructio S.C. de Religiosis, *Inter cetera*, 25 mart. 1956, II, 8 a), b), 9; III, 42 a), b)—*AAS*, XLVIII (1956), 514, 520.

[11] This is evident from the whole tenor of the Constitution *Sponsa Christi* and the Instruction *Inter cetera*.

[12] *Fontes*, n. 4412; *AAS*, IV (1912), 565-566.

[13] Instructio *Inter cetera*, II, n. 34—*AAS*, XLVIII (1956), 519.

[14] S.C. de Religiosis, 7 nov. 1916—*AAS*, VIII (1916), 446.

Therefore postulants as well as novices and professed nuns may not without apostolic permission leave the confines of the monastery observing the major papal cloister even for a short time or for any reason whatever except in the cases provided for in law.[15] These cases, if time permits, are to be previously authenticated by the local ordinary in writing; if not, he is to be informed afterwards of the departure from the cloister. The following cases receive mention: 1) Imminent danger of death, or a similar danger of serious evils, such as fire, flood, earthquake, a weakening of the building, a threatening collapse of the walls, air attacks, military invasion, and also the urgent requisition of the monastery by military or civil authority; 2) A grave and urgent surgical operation, or any other grave and urgent medical care required outside the cloister for the saving of life or the gaining of health, and a disease on the part of anyone that proves actually dangerous to the whole community; 3) The accompaniment or assistance rendered by the superioress or some duly deputed nun along with a companion nun to an extern sister in grave and urgent necessity outside the cloister, if otherwise such necessity cannot be afforded its needed relief.[16]

It is also permissible, after a declaration by the local ordinary, to go out of the cloister when it is obligatory to exercise civil rights or fulfill civil duties.[17]

The minor papal cloister entails a grave prohibition, for all and each of those subject to it, from going outside the limits of the monastery, just as the major cloister does for nuns and other persons who are bound by it. Dispensations from this grave prohibition may be given only for necessary reasons of the apostolate, and then only to those nuns and members who are legitimately assigned to the various tasks. The superioress may give nuns permission to go out for the reasons delineated in the particular constitutions or warranted by the law in general, but she is obliged in conscience to confine the use of this permission to the time during which the

[15] Canon 601, § 1.

[16] Canon 601, § 2; instr. *Inter cetera*, II, nn. 18, 21 a), b), c), d)—*AAS*, XLVIII (1956), 515, 516.

[17] Instr. *Inter cetera*, II, n. 22—*ibid.*, 516.

reasons certainly exist. For other reasons which are not expressly stated in law but clearly seem to be of equal import she is to recur to the local ordinary. The latter, after he has carefully considered the matter, may grant the permission, and may also authorize the superioress to grant it in the future. The there categories under which necessary services may afford a licit reason for the religious to go out are the following:

1) The needed accompaniment of girls in the promotion of study, the protection of health, or the supervision of recreation, when secular women teachers or auxiliaries are not available for a satisfactory performance of these duties;

2) The need of a due preparation for the efficient performance of their own work and services by means of an acquisition of knowledge and culture and a gaining of certificates and academic degrees through attendance at schools or colleges and a frequenting of conferences and congresses of learning;

3) Business affairs, legal matters, and similar items which with reference to the ecclesiastical and civil authorities, or in public or private offices, cannot safely and satisfactorily be handled by proxy.[18]

Although postulants for the religious habit, while they are serving their postulancy, are bound by the law of either the major or the minor cloister as outlined above, yet they may freely leave the monastery without the permission of the Holy See, or even of the local ordinary, when they decide of their own accord to return to the world, or are dismissed by their superiors.[19]

Although canon 540, § 3, states only that nun-postulants during the course of their postulancy are bound by the law of the cloister, it is quite clear that they are not permitted to leave the cloister after the completion of their postulancy either for a visit to their families or on the occasion of their clothing.[20]

---

[18] Instr. *Inter cetera,* III, nn. 50 a), b), c), d), 51 a), b), c)—*AAS,* XLVIII (1956), 522-523; canon 603.

[19] Instr. *Inter cetera,* II, n. 10—*ibid.,* 514.

[20] Instr. *Inter cetera,* II, n. 19—*ibid.,* 515; Schaefer, *De Religiosis,* n. 777.

Penalties

Briefly, the penalites for the violation of the papal cloister may be stated as follows: All nuns of solemn or simple vows, perpetual or temporary, who without permission go fully outside the major cloister or the confines of the monastery observing the minor cloister, but not those who go out licitly and then illegitimately remain outside, incur by that very fact an excommunication simply reserved to the Holy See. By an express concession of the Holy See, the excommunication for this species of crime in connection with the called for observance of the minor cloister may be reserved to the local ordinary instead of simply to the Holy See. The same penalty attaches to any person of whatever class, condition, or sex, who violates the major cloister or the parts of the house reserved to the community in monasteries observing the minor papal cloister, either by illegitimately entering therein or by illegitimately introducing or admitting others.[21] Nuns who are held to the observance of the minor cloister are according to the gravity of their guilt to be punished by their superioress or by the local ordinary if without at least the habitual or reasonably presumed permission of their superioress they leave the reserved quarters of the community for other places within the monastic precincts. Others who illegitimately enter these places, as well as those who introduce them or admit them, are to be severely punished according to the gravity of their act by the local ordinary of the place where the monastery is situated.[22]

Now it may be asked, do postulants who violate the cloister in the above mentioned ways incur these penalties? Since the issuance of the Instruction *Inter cetera* on March 25, 1956, it is quite clear that novices and postulants do not incur the excommunication leveled against those nuns who unlawfully go outisde the major papal cloister or the confines or precincts of a monastery observing the minor cloister.[23]

---

[21] Canon 2342, 1°, 3°; instr. *Inter cetera,* II, nn. 38, 39; III, nn. 60, 62 —*AAS,* XLVIII (1956), 519, 524.

[22] Instr. *Inter cetera,* III, nn. 61 a), b)., 63—*ibid.,* 524, 525.

[23] Instr. *Inter cetera,* II, n. 38—*AAS,* XLVIII (1956), 519. Cf. also *Sponsa Christi, Statuta Generalia,* art. I, § 1,—*AAS,* XLIII (1951), 15.

This had always been the common opinion of canonists in regard to the papal cloister defined by the Code, which corresponds to what is now designated as the major cloister. These authors held that novices and postulants were not to be considered as nuns (*moniales*) especially not in the matters of penal law, wherein a strict interpretation is called for. Likewise, they added, novices and postulants were not to be excommunicated for unlawfully taking leave of the cloister, for according to canon 2219, § 3, it is not permitted to extend a penalty from one class of persons to another, although a like or a more serious reason be present.[24] Some, however, did maintain that postulants incurred the excommunication for any unlawful departure from the cloister.[25]

But the penalties listed above in punishment of the introduction or admission of others into the major cloister or into places within a monastery observing minor cloister that lie within the community's proper quarters certainly may be incurred by postulants. Likewise postulants may incur all those penalties listed above in punishment of an unlawful entry, or the admission or introduction of others into those parts of the religious house which in a monastery observing the minor papal cloister are not reserved to the community. Hence, if a postulant without permission goes into a part of the monastery reserved for the work of the apostolate, or admits others to such a section of the monastery, she is to be reported by the superioress to the local ordinary, who will punish her according to the gravity of her action. Certainly the terminology used by the lawgiver in the Instruction *Inter cetera* will not allow one to concede to the postulants, who are

---

[24] Larraona, "Commentarium Codicis," *CpRM,* XVI (1935), 311; Schaefer, *De Religiosis,* n. 776; Coronata, *Institutiones,* I, n. 568; Ayrinhac, *Penal Legislation in the New Code of Canon Law* (New York: Benziger Bros., 1936), p. 267; Schaaf, *The Cloister,* The Catholic University of America Canon Law Studies, n. 13 (Washington, D. C.: The Catholic University of America, 1921), p. 144; Cerato, *Censurae Vigentes Ipso Facto a Codice Iuris Canonici Excerptae* (2. ed., Patavii: Typis Seminarii, 1921), 1251; Schweiger, "Quaestio Canonica," *CpR,* IV (1923), 140-145.

[25] Cf., e.g., Sole, *De Delictis et Poenis* (Rome-New York: Pustet, 1920), n. 374.

bound by the law of the cloister, more freedom in this regard than that which is allowed to outsiders.[26]

[26] This is evident from a study of those parts of the Instruction *Inter cetera* which are cited in footnotes 21, 22, and 23.

CHAPTER VIII

ADMISSION TO THE CANONICAL POSTULANCY

A. The Competent Superior

The Code is silent with regard to who is the proper superior competent for admitting candidates to the postulancy, and thus it leaves undetermined whether this right belongs to the major superior alone, or whether the local superior also is competent to receive postulants. Accordingly, one must look to special law to see whether the local superior is granted this faculty.[1] If, however, the special law is silent on this matter, it seems that the act of receiving postulants should be reserved to the major superior of the province, namely the provincial.

It seems to be in conformity with the nature of the candidate's request for admission into the institute that the major superior, who represents the institute more directly than the superior of an individual house, be held to admit the candidate.[2] This conclusion, too, is more in keeping with the earlier law, which saw the reception of new members into the community as a matter for the provincial's interest. Similarly, the acceptance of candidates into the novitiate devolves upon the major superior, and it is thus his duty to see that the candidates have the requisite qualities.[3] It appears to be the general practice to reserve the acceptance of candidates for the postulancy to the major superior.[4] In accepting

[1] Schaefer, *De Religiosis*, n. 771; Fanfani, *De Iure Religiosorum*, n. 190; O'Brien, *The Provincial Superior in Religious Orders of Men*, p. 85.

[2] Clancy, *The Local Religious Superior*, The Catholic University of America Canon Law Studies, n. 175 (Washington, D. C.: The Catholic University of America Press, 1943), p. 80; O'Brien, *loc. cit.*

[3] Larraona, "Commentarium Codicis," *CpRM*, XVI (1935), 226;' O'Brien, *loc. cit.*

[4] Beste, *Introductio in Codicem*, p. 363; Schaefer, *De Religiosis*, n. 771; Larraona," art. cit.," *loc. cit.*

candidates the major superior, as far as the common law is concerned, need not seek the advice or consent of his council or chapter. If a vote of the chapter should be required by special law, it will only be consultative.[5]

If an institute should have but one house, the superior of that house certainly enjoys the authority to receive the postulants; if the institute has many houses but is not yet divided into provinces, the superior general is the competent superior for granting admission to the postulancy.[6]

B. The Impediments to the Postulancy

Of the impediments which canon 542 lists as affecting the validity or the lawfulness of a candidate's entry into the novitiate, the writer believes that only those can be applied with equal force to one's admission to the postulancy which are either more accurate determinations of canon 538,[7] or from which by their very nature or in the practice of the Church dispensations are usually not granted.[8] This opinion is by no means held by all commentators, nor perhaps by even the majority of them. The view of the opposing authors will be discussed in due course. The above stated view, namely that postulants are not inherently (*ex se*) affected by all the impediments of canon 542, is the one espoused by Larraona,[9] Vermeersch,[10] Wernz-Vidal, and Schaefer,[11] among others.

In support of this position the following arguments may be adduced:

---

[5] Schaefer, *loc. cit.;* Larraona, "Commentarium Codicis," *CpRM,* XVI (1935), 227. Cf., e.g., *Constitutiones Ordinis Recollectorum Sancti Augustini,* n. 37, 4°.

[6] Schaefer, *De Religiosis,* n. 771; Fanfani, *De Iure Religiosorum,* n. 215.

[7] This canon allows any Catholic who is not barred by a legitimate impediment and who is inspired by the right intention and fit to bear the burdens of religious life to be admitted into religion.

[8] Larraona, "Commentarium Codicis," *CpRM,* XVI (1935), 223; Schaefer, *De Religiosis,* n. 764.

[9] "Commentarium Codicis," *CpRM,* XV (1934), 366; *CpRM,* XVI (1935), 223.

[10] *Periodica,* IX (1921), (5).

[11] *Ius Canonicum,* III, n. 240; *De Religiosis,* nn. 763, 764.

The clause "who is not debarred by any legitimate impediment," as used in canon 538, looks to the various impediments affecting the three types or grades of entry into religion, namely, to the postulancy, the novitiate and to profession. In other words, impediments which have been established with reference to a person's admission to the novitiate cannot in and of themselves (*ex se*) be extended to cover the cases of entry into the postulancy or of admission to religious profession. Without doubt, some of the impediments established by either the general or the special law for one of these three grades of entry into religion also apply to the others, but it is necessary to rely on interpretation, jurisprudence and pre-Code law in order to determine to what extent the impediments established with reference to one of these entries may be extended to the others. Having set down this principle, one must admit that almost all of the impediments applicable in canon 542 to admission to the novitiate must also be applied and indeed are so applied by most of the constitutions with reference to admission to the postulancy. The reason for this is that most of these impediments listed in canon 542 are in reality only more accurate determinations of the statement contained in canon 538, or are impediments from which by their very nature or in the practice of the Church dispensations are usually not granted.

Since the whole question of impediments may be certainly considered as something odious in law, and therefore something to be strictly interpreted and restricted as far as possible,[12] the impediments listed in canon 542 with reference to a valid or also a lawful entry into the novitiate should not in and of themselves (*ex se*) be extended to the postulancy.[13]

The true intention of canon 538 is to declare that fundamentally (*per se*) any Catholic may enter a religious community rather than to define accurately the impediments preventing such entry. Accordingly a complete transference to the postulancy of all the impediments that are listed in canon 542 with reference to admission to the novitiate, simply on the strength of the terminology

---

[12] Canon 19.

[13] Larraona, "Consultationes," *CpR*, I (1920), 181.

employed in canon 538, seems certainly unwarranted. It appears that the legislator did not want the impediments which are recounted in canon 542 to be applicable also for the postulancy from the very fact that the Code treats of the postulancy and the novitiate in different Chapters (I and II respectively) of Title XI. This conclusion, namely, that postulants are not affected by the impediments listed in canon 542, is applicable only to the impediments of positive ecclesiastical law for which dispensations are usually obtainable, and then only in so far as they affect worthy (*idonei*) Catholics. Non-Catholics and unworthy (*non-idonei*) Catholics may never be admitted to the postulancy, for they are expressly excluded by canon 538.[14] Larraona gives us the following division of impediments in regard to the postulancy.[15] The following are invalidly admitted to the postulancy: Catholics who have voluntarily joined a non-Catholic or atheistic sect; those who entered the postulancy under the influence of force, grave fear or fraud, or who were admitted by a superior thus constrained; married persons for the duration of their marriage; bishops whether residential or titular, even though only nominated by the Roman Pontiff; clerics who by a disposition of the Holy See are bound by oath to consecrate themselves to the service of their diocese or the missions, for the period during which their oath binds them.

Those who do not have the required age for admittance to the novitiate can be validly and lawfully admitted to the postulancy. It is evident, however, that the candidate's age must be such that when the postulancy is completed, he will be of an age that will allow him to make a valid entry into the novitiate according to the norms of canon 555. Thus a candidate who was born on the 4 of December, 1930, could not validly enter a novitiate according to the Code until the 5 of December, 1945, but he could validly and lawfully have entered the postulancy on the 4 of June, 1945, if the institute demanded a six-month postulancy.

There are other impediments, as for example the bond of a

---

[14] Vermeersch, "Quaestiones de Codice Canonico," *Periodica,* IX (1921), (5).

[15] "Commentarium Codicis," *CpRM,* XVI (1935), 223, nota (67).

former religious profession, which do not seem, in an absolute sense, to be impediments for the postulancy. Hence, a candidate who had once been a professed member of a religious institute could validly and lawfully enter the postulancy. Of course, a dispensation would have to be sought for such a postulant during the period of his postulancy in order that he might validly enter the novitiate. Naturally, this does not apply to the case of one who is still bound by the ties of a religious profession.

Before passing on to the canonists who maintain the opposing view, one should note here that Larraona seems to have modified his position somewhat in regard to one of the impediments listed above. In the *Commentarium pro Religiosis et Missionariis* for the year 1935, which was cited above, he was of the opinion that the postulancy of a candidate who enters it under the influence of grave fear, force or fraud, or who is admitted by a superior thus constrained, is invalid. Writing, however, in the same review for the following year[16] he stated that for the entry and admission to the postulancy the general principles of law were to be followed. Accordingly acts performed under the compulsion of an external force which cannot be resisted are to be considered null and void; acts performed under the influence of grave and unjustly inflicted fear, or of fraud, are valid unless the law provides otherwise, but can be annulled by the sentence of an ecclesiastical judge.[17]

To the writer, at least, this seems to be the correct view, for it is more in harmony with his basic opinion that postulants are not inherently (*ex se*) subject to the impediments of canon 542. In fact, for those who support this opinion, it appears to be the only defensible position in regard to this impediment (force-fear-fraud), in view of the wording of canon 103, § 2.

Concerning this impediment as well as all other impediments that are applicable to the postulancy, one must continually keep in mind that the invalidity of the postulancy by no means imports the invalidity of the subsequent novitiate. The postulancy is not required by the common law for the validity of the novitiate.

---

[16] "Commentarium Codicis," *CpRM,* XVII (1936), 12.

[17] Canon 103, §§ 1, 2.

Superiors, however, must be solicitous that candidates enter upon their postulancy validly. A superior who disregards the norms of the common law in regard to the postulancy could be guilty of grave fault.[18]

If because of an impediment a candidate has been admitted to the postulancy invalidly, his subsequent entry into the novitiate is not rendered invalid thereby, provided that the impediment has ceased or has been cancelled by means of a dispensation prior to his actual investiture in the habit of a novice.[19]

As was mentioned previously, there is another group of commentators, and perhaps the larger, which maintains that all the impediments of canon 542 as regards both validity and lawfulness should also be considered applicable to the postulancy. Among those who definitely support this view, or at least appear to favor it in their writings, are Prümmer,[20] Oesterle,[21] De Meester,[22] Ferreres[23] (1861-1936), Augustine,[24] Cocchi,[25] and Fanfani.[26]

These authors either expressly or by implication maintain that all the impediments listed in canon 542 should be extended to the postulancy because of the terminology of canon 538. This canon, which is concerned with every entry into religion, whether this be only to the postulancy, or to the novitiate or to profession, ab-

---

[18] Creusen, *Religious in the Code,* n. 177; Balzer, *The Computation of Time in a Canonical Novitiate,* p. 97. It might also be added that if the postulancy is prescribed by special law, the gravity of the fault must be determined by the binding power of the constitutions.

[19] Brown, *The Invalidating Effects of Force, Fear, and Fraud upon the Canonical Novitiate,* The Catholic University of America Canon Law Studies, n. 311 (Washington, D. C.: The Catholic University of America Press, 1951), pp. 50-51; Schaefer, *De Religiosis,* n. 770.

[20] *Manuale Iuris Canonici,* Q. 199, p. 266.

[21] *Praelectiones Iuris Canonici,* I (Romae: apud Collegium S. Anselmi, 1931), p. 282.

[22] *Juris Canonici et Juris Canonico-Civilis Compendium* (3 vols. in 4, Brugis: Desclée, 1921-1928; Vol. II, 1923), II, n. 985.

[23] *Institutiones Canonicae iuxta Codicem Novissimum* (2. ed., 2 vols., Barcinone, 1920), n. 847.

[24] *A Commentary on the New Code of Canon Law,* III, 198-199.

[25] *De Religiosis,* n. 60.

[26] *De Iure Religiosorum,* n. 179, B.

solutely demands that a candidate for a religious institute must be a Catholic, moved by the right motive, capable of bearing the burdens of the religious life, and not be barred by any legal impediment.[27] They add, however, that, since the Code in treating of the postulancy (canons 539-541) makes mention of no special impediments for admission to it, the general words of canon 538, which, as has been pointed out, apply to every type of entry into the religious life, seem to extend to the postulancy all the impediments which the Code treats of, not without reason, when legislating for the novitiate.

The assigned reason for its dealing with both the impediments for entering the novitiate and those for entering the postulancy in one and the same place (canon 542) is that for candidates who are destined for Holy Orders in clerical religious institutes, as also for candidates who will make profession of only temporary vows, no postulancy is required by the common law, and consequently such candidates may be admitted immediately into the novitiate. Hence the Code for the sake of convenience and order, has reserved its legislation on the impediments that bar valid and lawful entry into the religious life for that section in which it deals with the novitiate to which all religious without exception are bound.[28] Most, if not all, of the proponents of this opinion admit, however, that one may be validly and lawfully admitted to the postulancy even though he lack the required age for admission to the novitiate.

It appears from the foregoing brief exposition of the two schools of thought in reference to the impediments listed in canon 542 as they affect the postulancy that both seem to be intrinsically and extrinsically probable. After reviewing the various opinions in the foregoing discussion, one is tempted to conclude impartially that both contentions do not lack probability and that neither seems certain. Nevertheless, it appears to the writer that the better arguments derived from the law itself are in favor of the milder view. But it also seems that the present case is a perfect example of a

---

[27] Cf. canon. 538.

[28] Larraona, "Consultationes," *CpR,* I (1920), 181.

doubt of law, for the extent of the law in question is certainly shrouded in considerable doubt. Therefore, until such time that there is an authentic statement to the contrary, one is perfectly justified in applying here the principle of canon 15, that laws, even invalidating and disqualifying ones, have no binding force in the face of a doubt of law.

The foregoing discussion is, needless to say, of much greater speculative than practical value, since the postulancy is not required for a valid novitiate. Likewise the constitutions of individual religious institutes have almost universally legislated on this point more extensively and clearly than has the Code, and it is to these constitutions that one must look for the final word in any particular case. Nevertheless, the solution offered will not be totally devoid of practical application in those religious institutes whose constitutions are either silent or merely repeat the law of the Code on this point.

C. Testimonial Letters

While it is clear that the superior should not admit a candidate to the novitiate unless he has the testimonials specified in canon 544, the same cannot be said regarding the admission of a candidate to the postulancy. Certainly to forestall the possibility of future difficulties and the danger of delays when these documents are needed, it will be expedient and prudent for the superior to demand them from the beginning. Moreover, the special law of each institute may well require that these or similar documents be on hand before one is allowed to commence his postulancy.

Canon 538 demands for the admission into religion only that the candidate be baptized, loyal to the Faith, free from impediments, capable of assuming the burdens of religious life, and possessed of a right intention. The superior should ascertain through adequate investigations that the candidate possesses these requisite qualifications. For instance, the superior should insist on the presentation of certificates of baptism and confirmation.[29] Some authors maintain, however, that there is nothing to hinder the superior from

[29] Larraona, "Consultationes," *CpR,* I (1920), 179; Vermeersch, "Quaestiones de Codice Canonico," *Periodica,* IX (1921), (5).

accepting a postulant who has not yet been confirmed, provided he receives this sacrament during the course of his postulancy.[30]

It is true that canon 544, §§ 1, 2, and 6, when it demands testimonials for prospective novices, uses the term aspirants ("*adspirantes*"), which is frequently applied in general usage to postulants.[31] The general heading, however, of the chapter of the Code under which this canon is placed refers not to the postulancy but to the novitiate. Therefore the presumption should be that the application of this law is restricted to those who are about to be admitted into religion as novices, and is not extended to embrace those who are preparing for admission to the postulancy.[32] Moreover, this argument is not nullified in any way by the Code's use of the term "aspirant" in any specific sense, for the Code applies this term indiscriminately to novices and postulants alike.[33] Accordingly it may safely be said that the superior is not obliged to be in possession of these testimonials at the time of the admission of the candidate to the postulancy.[34] Furthermore, this opinion is in conformity with the earlier law,[35] which simply required that these testimonial letters be obtained prior to the time when the candidate was clothed with the religious habit, which normally took place at the beginning of the novitiate.

D. The Juridical Commencement of the Postulancy

According to the more common opinon, unless the constitutions furnish more definite regulations, the postulancy commences at the moment the candidate takes up residence in the religious house

---

[30] Larraona, *loc. cit.;* Schaefer, *De Religiosis,* n. 772; Goyeneche, *De Religiosis,* n. 44, nota (15).

[31] Cf., e.g., canon 540, § 3.

[32] Schaefer, *De Religiosis,* n. 772.

[33] Cf., e.g., canons 552 § 2; 570, § 2.

[34] Goyeneche, "Consultationes," *CpR,* VIII (1927), 33; Wernz-Vidal, *Ius Canonicum,* III, n. 244; Prümmer, *Manuale Iuris Canonici,* Q. 203, 6. Ferreres held the opposite opinion—*Institutiones Canonicae iuxta Codicem Novissimum,* I, n. 853.

[35] Decr. *Romani Pontifices,* 25 ian. 1848—Bizzarri, pp. 831-832; decr. 1 maii, 1851—Bizzari, pp. 839-843.

with the permission of the superior.[36] No special act or formality is required by the common law to mark the starting point of the postulancy.[37] It is left for the constitutions, however, to determine the precise way in which the postulancy it to be officially begun.[38]

Although the common law is silent on the matter of compensation for work done in the community by a postulant, superiors would do well, if the constitutions are equally silent on this point, to demand that prospective postulants before they begin their postulancy sign a document to the effect that they will exact no recompense from the institute for any work they performed during the postulancy in the event they should leave or be dismissed from the institute.[39]

---

[36] Fanfani, *De Iure Religiosorum,* n. 190; Berutti, *Institutiones,* III, n. 66, I; Vermeersch-Creusen, *Epitome,* I, n. 667; Coronata, *Institutiones,* I, n. 567; Wernz-Vidal, *Ius Canonicum,* III, n. 242; Schaefer, *De Religiosis,* n. 774.

[37] Cf. preceding footnote, especially Coronata, *loc. cit.* The writer, however, and Balzer (cf. *supra,* p. 84) are of the opinion that the clothing of the postulant with a modest garb distinct from that of the novices is set down in the Code by analogy as the point from which the postulancy should commence.

[38] Cf., e.g., *Caeremoniale Ordinis Recollectorum Sancti Augustini* (Romae, 1950), nn. 876, 877, where the rite of the private ceremony of investing the postulants with their proper habit is described.

[39] Schaefer, *De Religiosis,* n. 931; *Caeremoniale Ordinis Recollectorum Sancti Augustini,* n. 975, where the following form is suggested: I ...., ... years of age, the legitimate son of .... in the city of ....,in the state of .... located in the diocese of .... claim that of my own free-will I desire to be admitted into the Order (Society or Congregation) of ....; I also promise that I will serve in it without any reward and that I will demand no recompense if for any reason I shall in the future have to leave the Order (Society or Congregation).

Signed ....

Two witnesses who do not belong to the institute should also sign this document.

CHAPTER IX

THE MONETARY REQUIREMENTS OF THE CANONICAL POSTULANCY

A. The Dower Requirements

Canon 547, § 1, demands the payment of a dowry by postulants seeking to become members of a monastery of nuns.[1] Although the determination of the amount is left to the particular constitutions or to legitimate custom, the obligation of a dowry is imposed by the common law on postulants aspiring to membership in all monasteries of nuns.[2]

Since the Code, when prescribing the obligations of a dowry in monasteries of nuns, makes no distinction between prospective choir nuns and prospective lay nuns, the law must be considered as applying to both.[3] In regard to the amount, however, the constitutions or custom of the institute, as they frequently did in the older law, may require a dowry in smaller amount from the prospective lay nuns.

In virtue of canon 5, an immemorial custom of admitting non-choir postulants into a monastery of nuns without a dowry may be permitted to continue if the ordinary decides that it cannot be prudently abolished because of special circumstances.[4]

With reference to monasteries of nuns, special provisions have

---

[1] "In monasteriis monialium postulans afferat dotem in constitutionibus statutam aut legitima consuetudine determinatam."

[2] Coronata, *Institutiones*, I, n. 577; Wernz-Vidal, *Ius Canonicum*, III, n. 268; Vermeersch-Creusen, *Epitome*, I, n. 698; Vromant, *Ius Missionariorum*, Vol. VI, *De Bonis Ecclesiae Temporalibus* (Louvain: Museum Lessianum, 1927), n. 252, 1.

[3] Cf. Goyeneche, "Consultationes," *CpR*, XI (1930), 37; Vromant, *De Bonis Ecclesiae Temporalibus*, n. 252.

[4] Wernz-Vidal, *Ius Canonicum*, III, n. 268; Vermeersch-Creusen, *Epitome*, I, n. 698; Goyeneche, *loc. cit.*; Larraona, "Commentarium Codicis," *CpRM*, XX (1939), 80-81.

been made by the Holy See for the reception of extern sisters without a dowry. This class of sisters was introduced for the purpose of having someone to conduct the external affairs of the community. Special permission of the Holy See is required in each case to establish this class of religious. Their vows are simple, and they are not bound by the strict law of the cloister which obliges the nuns. In order to safeguard the religious life of the extern sisters, the Sacred Congregation of Religious published on July 16, 1931, with the approval of the Holy Father, a special list of statutes to be adopted and observed by these sisters. Article 51 forbids the requirement of a dowry, although it does state that the extern sisters should bring clothing and other furnishings according to the norms prescribed by the superioress of the monastery.[5] Cardinal la Puma (1874-1943), who was Secretary of the Sacred Congregation of Religious at that time, by way of commentary on Article 51, stated that a dowry must not be exacted from the extern sisters, nor should it even be mentioned, lest it lead to a double category of religious within this class. He added, however, that if an exern sister brought something like a dowry, the rules governing the dowry were to be observed. Although the statutes forbid the exaction of a dowry, so he said, they do not forbid the acceptance of one when it is offered.[6]

Immediately after imposing the obligation of a dowry in all monasteries of nuns the Code regulates the time and the manner in which the payment must be made. The dowry is to be given to the monastery before the prospective nun is clothed in the habit, or at least its payment is to be guaranteed in a form protected by civil law.[7] While these regulations are restricted to monasteries of nuns, the Sacred Congregation of Religious usually requires similar regulations to be inserted in the constitutions of congregations of sisters with simple vows, if the constitutions of

---

[5] S.C. de Religiosis, Statuta a sororibus externis monasteriorum monialium cuiusque ordinis servanda, 16 iul. 1931—*CpR,* XIV (1933), 167.

[6] Cf. *CpR, loc. cit.*

[7] Canon 547, § 2: "Haec dos ante susceptionem habitus monasterio tradatur aut saltem eius traditio tuta reddatur forma iure civili valida."

these sisters demand a dowry.[8] It remains for the constitutions of religious congregations of sisters with simple vows to insist upon or to waive the need of a dowry. Hence in the constitutions there may be required a dowry from all candidates indiscriminately, or only from the prospective choir sisters.[9]

By virtue, then, of canon 547, § 3, the constitutions of religious congregations can specify the optional regulations pertaining to the time and manner of payment, which matters are regulated for non-postulants in canon 547, §2.

The necessity, dictated by canon 547, § 2, for nuns, or by special law for sisters, of presenting the dowry before the beginning of the novitiate does not imply that the candidate must present it when she first takes up her life in the community. The law would be satisfied if the postulant supplied her dowry at any time before the expiration of the term of her postulancy. Nuns may present it in one sum, or in installments, provided the entire amount is in the hands of the institute before the reception of the habit.[10] In the event that the candidate does not make profession, the dowry must be returned.[11]

By way of summary, then, it may be said that nun-postulants are obliged to furnish a dowry to the monastery before they receive the habit of the novices. Sisters, on the other hand, must follow the provisions of their constitutions in regard to the necessity of the dowry as well as the time at which it must be handed over to the community. Although canon 551, § 1,[12] speaks of "professed religious," there can be no doubt about the obligation

---

[8] Coronata, *Institutiones,* I, n. 577; Vermeersch-Creusen, *Epitome,* I, n. 699; Jardi, *El Derecho de las Religiosas segun las Prescripciones Vigentes del Codigo Canonico y Civil* (2. ed., Vich: Serafica, 1927), p. 167, n. 450.

[9] Cf. canon 547, § 3; Vermeersch-Creusen, *Epitome,* I, n. 698; Oesterle, *Praelectiones Iuris Canonici,* I, 301; Toso, *Ad Codicem Iuris Canonici Commentaria Minora* (5 vols., Romae: Marietti, 1920-1927), Lib. II, pars II, p. 108, n. 4; Wernz-Vidal, *Ius Canonicum,* III, p. 223, n. 268; Bastien, *Directoire Canonique,* n. 99.

[10] Canon 553.

[11] Cf. canon 570, § 2.

[12] "Dos religiosae professae sive votorum solemnium sive votorum

of the institute to refund the dowry given by a postulant who departs without making her profession. For *a fortiori* the institute in such a case can make no claim whatsoever to the dowry. The money or securities which represent the dowry are merely on deposit, as it were, with the institute throughout the time of the postulancy. All rights of the institute to the dotal funds are conditioned on the future profession of the candidate.[13] The obligation of returning the dowry to a departing postulant arises even more from canon 570, § 2, than from canon 551, §1.[14] Canon 570, § 2, prescribes that, if the postulant leaves without making profession, she is to receive all possessions which she brought if they have not been consumed by use. With regard to this law, it makes no difference whether the postulant leaves voluntarily or whether she is dismissed by her superiors.

B. The Expenses of the Postulancy

Canon 570, §1,[15] states that no compensation may be claimed for the expenditures in keeping a postulant, except what the constitutions perhaps demand for food and clothing, or what was agreed upon for these purposes by explicit agreement at the beginning of the postulancy. Whatever is given to the community in accordance with this canon should not be confused with the dowry. It is entirely distinct from it. Its purpose is to defray the expenses of the postulancy, while the dowry consists in a capital sum, the income from which contributes to the support of the religious after profession.[16] Canon 570, § 1, makes no distinction

simplicium quavis de causa discedenti integra restituenda est sine fructibus iam maturis."

[13] Larraona, "Commentarium Codicis," *CpRM,* XXI (1940), 146; Kealy, *Dowry of Women Religious,* The Catholic University of America Canon Law Studies, n. 134 (Washington, D. C.: The Catholic University of America Press, 1941), pp. 108-109.

[14] Oesterle, *Praelectiones Iuris Canonici,* I, 302.

[15] "Nisi pro alimentis et habitu religioso in constitutionibus vel expressa conventione aliquid in postulatu vel novitiatu ineundo solvendum caveatur, nihil pro impensis postulatus vel novitiatus exigi potest."

[16] Cf. Larraona, "Commentarium Codicis," XX (1939), 10. Cocchi uses the word "dowry" in a broad and improper sense when he says that

between men and women religious and therefore applies to religious institutes of men as well as of women,[17] while the dotal law applies only to the latter.

The second paragraph of canon 570[18] demands that whatever the candidate brought to the institute, if it has not been consumed by use, must be returned if the postulant does not make profession and returns to the world. If the constitutions or custom requires the candidate to bring linens, clothing and similar equipment, a record of these articles should be kept, so that they may be returned if the candidate fails to make profession.[19] It is not correct to maintain, as Coronata[20] and Leitner[21] (1862-1929) did, that such articles for individual use can constitute a dowry. It is entirely lawful for the constitutions or custom to prescribe the bringing of these articles, which by their very nature are unproductive and consumed by use, but they should not be considered as a substitute for the dowry.[22] They fail to measure up to the nature and purpose of a dowry, and furthermore it would be impossible to observe in their regard the regulations concerning the dowry.[23]

By way of summary, then, it may be said that nun-postulants are obliged by the common law to furnish a dowry to the monastery before they receive the habit of the novices. On the other hand, sister-postulants must follow the provision of their own constitutions in regard both to the necessity of the dowry and to the time

---

many communities of sisters demand a dowry only for the support of the novice during the novitiate: "In multis religionibus sororum dos exigitur tantum pro sustentatione tempore novitiatus."—*De Religiosis,* II, p. 116, n. 67.

[17] Cf. canon 490.

[18] "Quae adspirans attulerit et usu consumpta non fuerint, si e religione, non emissa professione, egrediatur, ei restituantur."

[19] Wernz-Vidal, *Ius Canonicum,* III, n. 272; Schaefer, *De Religiosis,* n. 931.

[20] *Institutiones,* I, n. 577.

[21] *Handbuch des katholischen Kirchenrechts, Dritte Lieferung: Das Ordensrecht* (2. ed., Regensburg: Kosel and Pustet, 1922), p. 391.

[22] Larraona, "Commentarium Codicis," *CpRM,* XX (1939), 11, footnote 600.

[23] Cf. canons 549-551.

and manner in which it must be handed over to the community. Quite apart from the obligation of furnishing a dowry is the obligation incumbent on male as well as on female candidates for the religious life to furnish any sum prescribed by the constitutions for food and clothing during the postulancy. If the constitutions are silent, the institute may make an agreement on this point at the beginning of the postulancy. The dowry, however, as well as anything brought but unconsumed by use must be returned in the event that the candidate leaves the institute.

CHAPTER X

THE GOVERNMENT OF THE CANONICAL POSTULANCY

A. The Discipline of the Postulancy

The discipline of the postulancy is left to the judgment and discretion of the superior, unless the constitutions make specific provisions to the contrary.[1] It should be remembered, however, that postulants are neither novices nor religious, and therefore should not be subject to the restrictions imposed on either class.

On the other hand, Schaefer[2] pointed out that throughout the entire course of the postulancy there must be avoided those things which might offer the postulants an occasion of losing their vocation. There is no objection to the practice of having the postulants perform some external works of the society or of engaging in study.[3] Prudence, however, requires that a postulant should not be busily occupied in such pursuits to the extent that there would be a tendency for discouragement or even a risk of the privation of ample time for the proper performance of the exercises required of postulants.

According to Vermeersch-Creusen, postulants may be allowed to pursue their studies, even with lay students, provided: 1) that they live in a house of regular observance of the institute; 2) that they can be distinguished from the lay students by their garb, and 3) that they are under the care of an experienced religious who will guide them in the performance of their proper religious exercises.[4]

---

[1] Larraona, "Commentarium Codicis," *CpRM,* XVI (1935), 312, III; Schaefer, *De Religiosis,* n. 765; Vermeersch-Creusen, *Epitome,* I, n. 668.

[2] *De Religiosis* n. 763.

[3] Larraona, "Commentarium Codicis," *CpRM,* XVI (1935), 312, III; Creusen, *Religious in the Code,* n. 173.

[4] *Epitome,* I, n. 668.

Postulants who are preparing for the life of extern sisters in monasteries of nuns may be employed in domestic duties, but they must attend all the exercises of these sisters. They should not, however, be allowed to perform such duties as will require their making frequent visits into the city, and they must always be accompanied on such trips by a professed sister.[5]

During the period of the postulancy, the candidates for the religious life are subject to the various superiors of the institute, namely: the local superior; the provincial superior; and the general superior. Although they have not made religious profession, they have either explicitly or implicitly contracted of their own free will to obey these superiors.[6] The act of profession is not necessary for one to become included under the scope of the dominative power of these superiors. This power of the superior extends to them in virtue of a pact or implicit contract, for they have submitted themselves to the community. Of course, they are not bound to render their submission by reason of the virtue of religion, and they are free to leave the community at will; but as long as they remain in the institute they are obliged to submit to the authority of their superior by reason of the virtue of obedience. When they have left the community, they are no longer subject to this power.[7]

Besides this dominative power which the superiors of all institutes exercise over their postulants, the superiors of exempt clerical institutes also exercise jurisdictional power over postulants in the cases mentioned in the common law. Thus in virtue of the jurisdictional power attached to the office of the proper superior, postulants may be dispensed from the common law of fast and abstinence and from the observance of feasts or from both.[8] They

---

[5] S. C. of Religious, July 16, 1931, n. 23—*Apollinaris,* IV (1931), 348.

[6] Wernz-Vidal, *Ius Canonicum,* III, n. 93; Vermeersch-Creusen, *Epitome,* I, n. 619; Clancy, *The Local Religious Superior,* p. 38; Bowe, *Religious Superioresses,* The Catholic University of America Canon Law Studies, n. 228 (Washington, D. C.: The Catholic University of America Press, 1946), p. 66.

[7] Bowe, *Religious Superioresses,* p. 79.

[8] Canon 1245, § 3.

may be dispensed according to canons 1313, 2°, and 1320, from private non-reserved vows and from promissory oaths. The superior can also administer Viaticum and extreme unction to a sick postulant, in virtue of canon 514, § 1, since a postulant is understood to dwell in the religious house day and night *causa educationis*.[9] It is likewise the right of the superior (local or major, depending upon the constitutions) to confer delegated power to priests for the hearing of the confessions of the postulants.[10] On the other hand, if a postulant were to die in the course of the postulancy, the rules governing the burial of the faithful apply, and he would be buried from his parish church, unless he had made some other choice in this regard during life.[11] The superior, therefore, does not enjoy the same rights in the matter of the burial of the postulants as he does with respect to the novices and the professed,[12] and also of those who while living within the monastic premises are engaged in the actual service of the community.[13]

B. The Examination of Female Postulants Prior to the Novitiate

The Code does not prescribe any examination of the candidates before they are admitted to the postulancy. At least two months in advance of the reception of the novices into the novitiate in communities of women religious, the bishop must be informed, so that he can proceed personally or by means of a delegate to make a canonical examination of the candidates. This examination should be made at least one month before the ceremony of investiture.[14]

---

[9] If the postulant is confined outside the religious house by reason of illness, the superior does not have this right. Cf. Pontificia Commissio Interpretationis (PCI), 16 iun. 1931—*AAS,* XXIII (1931), 353. Cf. also *infra.* pp. 129-130.

[10] Canon 875, § 1.

[11] Canon 1222.

[12] Canon 1221, §§ 1, 2; cf. PCI, iul. 20, 1929, IV—*AAS,* XXI (1929), 573.

[13] Canon 1221, § 3.

[14] Canon 552.

Its purpose is solely to verify whether the postulant is acting with full knowledge and liberty. The bishop or his delegate may, therefore, without entering the papal cloister, question the postulant about her knowledge of the essential obligations of the religious life, about the three vows of religion, and the particular observances of the institute. The bishop merely permits the admission of the postulant to the novitiate, but he does not examine the postulant as to her vocation.[15] His authority is restricted in this examination to a veto based on his finding improper motives in the postulant, or a lack of freedom of choice in consequence of compulsion or fraud, and it is to the discovery of these dispositions that his examination must be limited.[16]

If the local ordinary, though informed, fails to comply with the requirements of this canon (552), the superioress may proceed to admit the postulants without further ado.[17]

C. Catechetical Instruction and Sermons for the Postulants

According to canon 509, § 2, 2°,[18] an instruction in Christian doctrine is to be given twice a month to the lay brothers and to the "*familiares*" (domestic servants), and a pious exhortation is to be given twice a month to all the members of the religious family, especially in lay religious institutes.

The writer holds that the term "*familiares*" of this canon comprehends only those who dwell day and night in the house of religious as domestic servants (*causa famulatus*).[19] This opinion is also supported by others.[20] Other commentators, however, would

---

[15] Creusen, *Religious in the Code,* n. 190.

[16] Coronata, *Institutiones,* I, n. 578.

[17] Vermeersch-Creusen, *Epitome,* I, n. 703; Beste, *Introductio in Codicem,* at canon 552.

[18] "Curent Superiores locales ut saltem bis in mense, firmo praescripto can. 565, § 2, christianae catechesis habeatur instructio pro conversis et familiaribus, audientium conditioni accommodata, et, praesertim in religionibus laicalibus, pia ad omnes de familia exhortatio."

[19] Schaefer, *De Religiosis,* n. 539.

[20] Cf. Larraona, "Commentarium Codicis," *CpR,* VIII (1927), 127 ff.; Vermeersch-Creusen, *Epitome,* I, n. 629.

extend this term so that it would include also those who are in the religious house day and night as students, guests, and patients.[21] Hence, according to this second group of authors, there would certainly seem to be an obligation on the superior to see that the postulants receive a catechetical instruction at least twice a month, for postulants appear to be among those who are present in the religious house *causa educationis.* Nevertheless, there is, in the opinion of the writer, sufficient weight of opinion to the contrary, so that it seems permissible to exclude postulants from the need of attending the bi-weekly instructions in Christian doctrine which the Code prescribes for lay brothers and domestic servants.

The phrase "*omnes de familia*" in canon 509 certainly includes only the true members of the religious community, and hence also the postulants. The servants and employees who live habitually within the religious house are not comprised within this phrase.[22]

Some writers, however,[23] would include these servants and employees in the religious family, and so according to them the postulants, with greater reason, would come also within the ambit of this phrase.

The subject matter of these exhortations may well be taken from that recommended in the documents which formed the basis of this canon.[24] It will generally regard matters of regular discipline and the acquisition of virtue. The superior may give these conferences personally or may ask others to do so. This exhortation should not consist merely of spiritual reading, unless this is

---

[21] Creusen, *Religious in the Code,* n. 87; Coronata, *Institutiones,* I, n. 540; Beste, *Introductio in Codicem,* at canon 509, § 2, 2°; Ramos, "De Conditione Saecularium in Domibus Religiosorum," *CpR,* VI (1925), 136, 140, 326.

[22] Schaefer, *De Religiosis,* n. 539; Ramos, "De Conditione Saecularium in Domibus Religiosorum," *CpR,* VI (1925), 324; Fanfani, *De Iure Religiosorum,* n. 441, B.

[23] Creusen, in n. 72 of the translation of the 4th edition of his French Work (*Religious in the Code,* [Milwaukee: Bruce, 1921]), and seemingly also, but not so strongly, in n. 87 of the Third English edition, which is a translation of the Fifth French edition.

[24] Clemens VIII, decr. *Nullus omnino,* 25 iul. 1599, § 25—*Fontes,* n. 187; S. C. Ep. et Reg., decr. 22 aug. 1814, n. XI—*Fontes,* n. 1893.

the only feasible arrangement.[25] In lay institutes the obligation of the sermon or conference is a grave one, which does not seem to be the case in clerical institutes.[26]

From what has been said above, it appears that postulants need not be present at the catechetical instruction that canon 509 calls for, since they are not classed as *familiares*; on the other hand, they are to attend the fortnightly sermons or conferences ordered by the same canon, for they belong to the religious family.

Beyond the provisions regarding religious instruction and exhortation as found in the law of the Code, the Sacred Congregation of Religious has issued an Instruction to the Superiors and Superioresses General of lay religious institutes on the knowledge of Christian doctrine that must, under their diligent care, be imparted to their subjects.[27] In this Instruction the following point is stressed in regard to the postulancy: during the postulancy and the novitiate, Christian doctrine shall be reviewed and learned thoroughly, so that each one will not only know it by heart but also be able to explain it correctly, and the novices shall not be admitted to take vows without a sufficient knowledge thereof, which shall be verified by means of a previous examination. This examination must show that their knowledge of the subject consists in an intellectual grasp of the truths of religion with a sufficient understanding to explain them correctly. The Sacred Congregation pointed out that the duty of learning this doctrine thoroughly is especially incumbent upon those who are consecrated to God in religious congregations: for without the knowledge of Christian doctrine they neither can nourish their own spiritual life as they should, nor can they labor for the salvation of others according to their vocation. The examination in this matter should be determined by the superior and be conducted by him or his delegate. If the superiors of lay religious institutes are to comply with this decree of the Holy See, they certainly must provide for frequent

[25] Coronata, *Institutiones,* I, n. 540; Schaefer, *De Religiosis,* n. 539.

[26] Coronata, *Institutiones,* I, *loc. cit.*

[27] *Ad supremos moderatores et moderatrices Religiosorum laicarum familiarum de obligatione subditos in doctrina Christiana rite imbuendi,* 25 nov. 1929—*AAS,* XXII (1930), 28-29.

instructions in Christian doctrine for their novices and postulants. Although the time interval between these instructions is not determined by this decree, it is evident from the tenor of this papal document that they will have to be held quite often. Canon 565, § 2, which orders that *conversi* novices must be carefully instructed in Christian doctrine at least once a week, may serve as an analogy in this matter, and hence these instructions for postulants in lay institutes should also be held weekly.[28]

This regulation applies only to the postulants of lay religious institutes, but it seems to include both the choir and lay religious, since the decree does not specify otherwise.

Although the Code and subsequent decrees do not bind superiors of clerical institutes to instruct *conversi* postulants as such[29] in Christian doctrine, it seems that they have an obligation to do so. The decree *Sacrosancta* of the Sacred Congregation for Religious,[30] which was neither abrogated nor derogated by the silence of canons 539-541, and the decree of November 25, 1929, reminded these superiors of their serious obligation in this regard. Concerning *conversi* postulants and novices the decree *Sacrosancta* stated:

> In accord with the decrees of the Holy See, they (superiors) shall explain all of *Christian doctrine*, and especially what pertains to the proper and fruitful reception of the sacraments of Penance and Holy Communion, using as their guide the Catechism of the Council of Trent for pastors. At the same time they shall teach them the obligations they will assume at religious profession and the virtues they must cultivate to lead the life of the vows. . . . (Writer's Italics).[31]

Pope Pius XI (1922-1939) likewise urged this obligation in his exhortation to all superiors of religious communities of men in his Apostolic Letter *Unigenitus* on March 19, 1924:[32]

---

[28] Fanfani, *De Iure Religiosorum*, *n.* 198, B.

[29] Those who are in lay religious institutes come under the instruction and the decree here mentioned. Cf. S. C. de Religiosis, 25 nov. 1929—*AAS*, XXII (1930), 28-29.

[30] Decree *Sacrosancta*, 1 ian. 1911—*Fontes*, n. 4407.

[31] *Fontes*, n. 4407.

[32] *AAS*, XVI (1924), 146-147.

> We shall now consider those religious who, although they are not called to the priesthood, nevertheless take the same religious vows as priests, and are therefore no less bound before God and held to the duty of striving after perfection. . . . We cannot refrain here, dearly beloved sons, from exhorting you to reflect on what a grave duty you have of watching that the *conversi*, both during their *time of probation* (*cum probationis tempore*) and throughout their lives, be furnished with the spiritual helps they need to advance and persevere, the need of these helps being perhaps the greater in proportion to the lowliness of their status and the humble work they have to do. . . . But most of all the superiors are not to neglect the *instruction of the lay brothers*, either personally or through priests who are properly qualified, *in the eternal and sublime truths of the faith*, which if known and frequently called to mind furnish many incentives to virtue for any man, whether living in the world or within the walls of a monastery. . . . (Writer's translation and Italics).

It is evident, then, from the two documents quoted above that superiors must provide instructions in Christian doctrine for their *conversi* postulants. Indeed, since canon 509, §2, 2°, requires it for the professed *conversi*, and canon 565, § 2, prescribes it for the *conversi* novices, the analogy in law would also indicate its necessity for the postulants. The mind of the legislator seems to be that the instruction of *conversi* must always be carefully provided for, and most especially during their time of probation. Certainly, then, it seems inconceivable that one admit that their instruction during the course of the postulancy, which, too, is a period of probation, may be neglected.

D. Administration of the Sacraments to the Postulants: Privileges

1. *Viaticum and Extreme Unction*

Canon 514, § 1, states that superiors of clerical institutes have the right and duty to administer personally or through another the sacraments of Holy Viaticum and extreme unction in the case of dangerous illness on the part of the professed, of the novices and of others who live day and night in the religious house to render service, to receive education, to share hospitality, or to recover their health. This includes, therefore, servants, pupils, guests, and patients.[33]

The superior's authority in reference to the administration of Viaticum and extreme unction to his own professed subjects and to the novices presents no difficulties as long as they are ill within the religious house.[34] When they are confined in a hospital outside the religious house, he still has the right to administer these two sacraments to these subjects;[35] but if he wishes to carry Viaticum *publicly* he must have at least the presumed permission of the pastor of the territory.[36] For the private administration of the Holy Eucharist to his subjects outside the religious house the superior needs only the permission of the priest in charge of the custody of the Blessed Sacrament at the church from which the superior wishes to take It.[37]

With regard to the clerical superior's authority over the lay and clerical postulants who are his subjects, it may be asked whether or not they are included among those mentioned in canon 514, § 1, in view of the fact that they are not expressly mentioned in the canon. Beyond doubt they are to be included, if they can be classed in one or the other of the four categories mentioned in that canon.[38] Pejška (1870-1946) held that postulants are equivalent to servants,[39] and Toso (+1946) that they are like to guests.[40] Many authors considered postulants as sharing at least to a degree in the privileges and favors granted to the religious institute. Accordingly they even extended to them the privileges granted

---

[33] "In omni religione clericali ius et officium Superiorbus est per se vel per alium aegrotis professis, novitiis, aliisve in religiosa domo diu noctuque degentibus causa famulatus aut educationis aut hospitii aut infirmae valetudinis, Eucharisticum Viaticum et extremam unctionem ministrandi."

[34] Augustine, *A Commentary on the New Code of Canon Law,* III, 142.

[35] Cf. PCI, 16 iun. 1931—*AAS,* XXIII (1931), 353; Vermeersch, "Annotationes," *Periodica,* XXI (1932), 38.

[36] Cf. canon 848, § 1.

[37] Cf. canon 848, § 2; Clancy, *The Local Religious Superior,* p. 138.

[38] Clancy, *The Local Religious Superior,* pp. 140-141.

[39] *Ius Canonicum Religiosorum,* p. 87.

[40] *Commentaria Minora,* II, Pars II, 56.

to novices in canon 567, §1, that is, all the privileges and spiritual favors granted to the institute.[41] The reasons for their extension of privileges to the postulants apparently were the following:

1) Postulants can be called religious in a broad sense, since they belong, although in a very unsettled and unstable way, to the religious family, and are under the immediate direction of the superiors of the religious institute, and often are clothed with a distinctive religious garb.

2) Postulants participate in the rights of novices in some matters. For example, the superior who has dominative power over their will may validly and also, for a justifying reason, lawfully annul their vows in such a way that their obligation never subsequently revives. Likewise the superior of an exempt clerical institute may for a justifying reason dispense from their vows if they are not reserved, provided the dispensation does not infringe on the vested rights of others.[42]

3) According to canon 540, §3, postulants in monasteries of nuns are bound to the observance of the law of the papal cloister in the same manner as the professed nuns.

This opinion has lost much of its value in view of an official interpretation of the Pontifical Commission, in which it was stated that the provision in canon 1221, in which reference is made to the burial of professed religious, novices, and servants, is not to be extended to postulants.[43] From this response, of course, it is certain only that postulants are not subject to the authority of the superior in regard to burial rights. The Commission was not asked to decide the question whether postulants share generally in the favors and privileges granted to religious, but the response given does indicate that it is hardly the mind of the Commission that postulants participate in privileges and favors granted to the professed religious and novices. In view of the response of the Commission, one should

---

[41] Maroto, "Annotationes," *CpR,* X (1919), 337-338. Coronata (*Institutiones,* I, n. 587) still believes that this opinion is not improbable.

[42] Cf. canons 1312, § 1, and 1313, 2°.

[43] PCI, 20 iul. 1929, IV— *AAS,* XXI (1929), 573.

conclude that postulants do not share in the other favors and privileges, unless they too are expressly mentioned.[44]

It is the writer's opinion that both apostolic students and postulants are certainly subject to the authority of the superior mentioned in canon 514, § 1, if they can be included under those who reside in the religious house *causa educationis*.[45] Postulants ought to be regarded as certainly in this category, and likewise those who are known as apostolic students, if they dwell in the religious house over night. They are better classified in this manner than among the group of servants or guests, inasmuch as the latter live in the religious house *causa famulatus aut hospitii*, and represent a class entirely distinct from those who are aspiring to admission in the institute. While not all the students are always postulants, all the postulants are certainly students of the religious life, which they seek to embrace later as novices and as professed religious.[46] Hence it is neither necessary nor advisable to consider postulants as included in the term *novitiis* of canon 514, § 1, or as guests or servants. They can simply be considered as students subject to the authority of the superior, and can be included among those who dwell in the religious house habitually *causa educationis*.

Although the expression "day and night" (*diu noctuque*) might imply a period of time protracted over several days and nights, authors consider it as relating to a privilege and accordingly subject it to a broad interpretation. They maintain, consequently, that residence in the religious house for a full day suffices to bring one under the authority of the superior indicated in canon 514. In fact, not even an actual residence for a 24-hour period seems to

---

[44] Schaefer, *De Religiosis*, n. 770; Larraona maintains the opposite opinion, namely, that one may still continue to apply to postulants the privileges granted to the professed religious. Cf. "Commentarium Codicis," *CpRM*, XVI (1935), 224, III.

[45] Clancy, *The Local Religious Superior*, p. 141. This is also the classification chosen by Berutti, though in addition he considers that postulants are equivalent to novices, for the application of canon 514, § 1. —*Institutiones*, III, n. 27.

[46] Clancy, *The Local Religious Superior*, p. 142.

be demanded, provided the subject has the intention of staying that long a time.[47]

Up to this point the matter under consideration has been the administration of Viaticum and extreme unction by the local superior to the postulants in the religious house. As was pointed out above in regard to the administration of Viaticum to the professed religious and novices, the Pontifical Commission declared that the authority given to the religious superior in canon 514, § 1, applied to these individuals even when they were confined outside of the religious house. Although the Commission had been asked whether the superior had the right to administer to all the persons mentioned in canon 514, § 1, when they were confined outside the religious house,[48] its answer affirmed such authority in regard to novices and professed alone. As for the others, it declared that those who resided in the religious house "*diu noctuque . . . causa famulatus aut educationis aut hospitii aut infirmae valetudinis*" were excluded from the superior's competence when they fell ill outside the religious house. Therefore, servants, students, guests and patients, when confined outside the religious house, are subjects of the pastor of the place in which they reside (unless a particular institute is entrusted to a chaplain).[49]

This decision of the Pontifical Commission accordingly excludes postulants from the competence of the local superior, if they are ill outside the religious house, at least if postulants are not understood as included also whenever reference is made in juridical documents to novices. It has already been shown that postulants are subject to the power of the local superior when they are present within the religious house, since they are present for the purpose of education (*causa educationis*). In view, therefore, of the reply of the Pontifical Commission, it should be clear that the local superior cannot administer Viaticum and extreme unction to postulants who are ill outside the religious house, unless he obtains the

---

[47]Augustine, *A Commentary on the New Code of Canon Law,* III, on Canon 514; Vermeersch-Creusen, *Epitome,* I, n. 632; Coronata, *Institutiones,* I, n. 540 ff.

[48] PCI, 16 iun. 1931—*AAS, XXIII* (1931), 353.

[49] Cf. canons 848, 850; "Annotationes," *Periodica,* XXI (1932), 38.

permission of the pastor or the particular priest who has been granted parochial rights in the place where the postulants are confined.[50]

In the case of the nun-postulants and of postulants in lay institutes the right to administer these two sacraments pertains to the ordinary confessor and the parish priest respectively when these postulants are ill within the religious house. If the lay institute, however, has been withdrawn from the jurisdiction of the local pastor, this right belongs to its chaplain, or to him who has received authorization to confer these sacraments. The authority however may be delegated to others.[51] If such postulants are ill outside the religious house, the local pastor or the duly authorized priest is the competent one in this regard.[52]

By way of conclusion to this discussion it may be stated that postulants are not strictly to be classified either as religious or as novices. Moreover, they should not to be considered as sharing in all the privileges and favors granted to the religious institute, as is indicated by the response of the Commission for the Authentic Interpretation of the Code.[53]

2. *Confessions of the Postulants*

The canons of the Code which deal with the confessors for the various classes of religious do not pertain directly to the postulants. Although those things which are prescribed for the confessions of novices (canons 526-527) may be conveniently adapted for the postulants, it must be remembered that they are not bound to these regulations of the common law, for in this matter they are equivalent to lay people.[54] Hence there is no special faculty required in order that one may hear the confessions of

[50] Clancy, *The Local Religious Superior,* pp. 143-144.

[51] Creusen, *Religious in the Code,* n. 150.

[52] Cf. canon 514, §§ 2, 3. In the case of necessity, e.g., if the pastor is absent, unable to act, etc. or if the pastor's permission can be reasonably presumed, any priest may validly and licitly administer extreme unction.—Cf. canon 938, § 2.

[53] *Supra,* p. 128.

[54] Larraona, "Commentarium Codicis," *CpRM,* XVI (1935), 312.

even women postulants.[55] The law of the cloister, however, to which the postulants are bound by either the common or the special law, may make it almost obligatory that they go to confession to the ordinary confessors of the house. Of course, if they have the lawful opportunity, they may go to confession, even habitually, to other priests. The necessity of spiritual direction, however, demands that they make some choice of a regular confessor.[56]

The law apparently desires to keep separate the internal and external forums. Since the postulants are his subjects, it is desirable that a superior who possesses faculties to hear confessions should hear the confessions of only those postulants who spontaneously and voluntarily approach him for this purpose. To make a habit of this the superior would require a serious justifying reason.[57]

The Pontifical Commission for the Authentic Interpretation of the Code stated on September 29, 1918, that the provisions of canon 518, § 2, must be observed by superiors in regard to the student subjects who form a section somewhat distinct from the community.[58] The writer has not been able to find an official publication of this response.[59] Yet, even if one were to conclude that it does not, therefore, bind, it is, nevertheless, an indication of the mind of the legislator on the matter. Accordingly, one could justifiably conclude from the law and this private response that superiors should not habitually hear the confessions of postulants who are subject to them.

The serious justifying reason which may permit a superior law-

---

[55] Schaefer, *De Religiosis,* n. 634.

[56] Creusen, *Religious in the Code,* n. 103.

[57] Canon 518, § 2; Goyeneche, *De Religiosis,* n. 25, II and note 12; *CpR,* XIV (1933), 259 ff; Vermeersch-Creusen, *Epitome,* I, n. 638, 6; Bcste, *Introductio in Codicem,* at canon 518, § 2; Larraona, "Consultationes," *CpR,* I (1920), 55, b.

[58] The words of the Commission are: "Quoniam Studentes partem a Communitate aliquo modo seiunctam efformant, respectu eorum observandus est can. 518, § 2.

[59] It is quoted in *Linzer-theologisch-praktische Quartalschrift,* Linz, LXXIV (1921), 439.

fully to hear the confessions of a postulant is required only when it is a habitual practice that is involved; in the absence of a habitual practice, the only condition required by the law is that the subject approach the superior spontaneously.[60] Illustrations of serious justifying reasons would be the following: emotional difficulty in confessing to other available priests; the handicap of difficulty with the confessor's language.[61]

Canon 891 states that the master of novices or his assistant should not ("*ne audiant*") hear the confessions of their subjects living in the same house, unless subjects spontaneously request it for a serious and urgent reason. This canon, however, is hardly to be extended to postulants, so that the novice master or his assistant would be forbidden to hear their confessions. Since this canon does not forbid the master of novices or his assistant to hear the confessions of the professed or others who are not novices, it seems unwarranted to exclude postulants from their sacramental guidance. Moreover, the prohibition is made regarding novices in the strict sense of the word. Hence, neither postulants nor the newly professed who may still be subject to the master of novices are comprehended under it.[62]

It is the opinion of the writer that the prefect of postulants may act as confessor for the postulants, unless this is forbidden by speical law, or unless authority over the students in the external forum is entrusted to him. But according to the general law itself there is nothing that bars the prefect of postulants from hearing the confessions of the postulants. This opinion is supported by the following reasons: 1) his functioning in this capacity is not forbidden by the *law* of the Code; 2) nor is it contrary to the *mind* of the legislator, and 3) the opinion is approved by the authority of canonists.

1) Religious superiors are forbidden in the Code (canon 518, § 2) to hear the confessions of their religious subjects, unless the

60 Larraona, "Consultationes," *CpR*, I (1920), 56; Coronata, *Institutiones*, I, n. 544.

61 Larraona, *loc. cit.;* Coronata, *loc. cit.;* Beste, *Introductio in Codicem,* at canon 518, § 2.

62 Larraona, "Commentarium Codicis," *CpRM,* XXV (1944), 11.

latter of their own free will request it. Further, the Code also requires that if the religious choose to confess habitually to their superiors, a serious cause must be present. In like manner the Code (canon 891) forbids the master of novices and his assistant to receive the sacramental confessions of their subjects who reside in the same house with them, unless the latter seek it of their own accord, and allows it then only for a grave and urgent reason and in particular cases.

The prefect of postulants is not comprehended within the ambit of the prohibition of either canon. He does not fall under the law enacted in canon 518, § 2, because he is not a superior in the strict sense as contemplated in this canon. The term is not extended to others who may even possess some authority in the external rule of the community, but is limited to the major and minor superiors. It does not include the prefect of postulants.[63] Neither is the prefect of postulants to be identified with those who are mentioned in canon 891, namely the master of novices or his assistant, although he may perform duties in some respects similar to the duties performed by these individuals. He is therefore, not forbidden by the Code to hear the confessions of the postulants either in a particular case, or even habitually.

2) It is not contrary to the mind of the legislator that the prefect of postulants act as confessor for the postulants. Throughout the Code there is a distinct separation of the external and internal forums in religious institutes, which is upheld in both theory and practice.[64]

The master of novices has authority in the external forum, and hence it is the expected thing that he should be explicitly excluded from exercising authority in the internal sacramental forum. Likewise the major and minor superiors have the government in the external forum entrusted to them. The legislator, in order to preserve the separation of forums, allows religious to confess to their superiors only under certain conditions. The prefect of postulants is not entrusted, at least by the common law, with the external

---

[63] Larraona, "Consultationes," *CpR,* I (1920), 54, 55.

[64] Cf. canons 518, § 2; 530; 891.

government of the postulants. As a consequence it is not contrary to the mind of the legislator for the prefect of postulants to hear the confessions of the postulants, for he does not exercise authority in the external forum, according to the common law.[65]

3) It is the opinion of the authors that the prefect of postulants is not forbidden by the common law to act as confessor for the postulants. Larraona says that the prefect of postulants is not embraced in the prescriptions of canon 891. The reason he gives is that the external discipline is not necessarily entrusted to the prefect of postulants by the common law as it is in the case of the master of novices. Nevertheless, he admits that sometimes from the special law the external discipline is included in the charge of the prefect. In such an instance the prefect of postulants is more like a superior than a master of novices.[66]

Other authors[67] do not treat precisely of this question. They all agree, however, that the spiritual prefect is not forbidden by the common law to act as confessor of the students subject to him. Hence, to the writer at least, it seems logical to conclude that they would be of the same opinion in regard to the prefect of postulants, since the two offices bear a marked similarity one to the other.

Since the appearance in 1956 of the Apostolic Constitution *Sedes Sapientiae* and the *General Statutes* annexed to it, the opinion of those authors who held that the common law did not forbid the spiritual prefect to act as confessor for the students subject to him is no longer tenable. In article 28, § 2, 10°, this Constitution states:

> The prescriptions of canon 891 concerning the master of novices being observed, the spiritual prefect or master, since he necessarily takes part in the final evaluation conducted be-

[65] Cf. canon 540, § 1.

[66] Larraona, "Commentarium Codicis," *CpRM,* XXV (1944), 11, 12, nota (1205).

[67] Berutti, *Institutiones,* III, n. 100; Coronata, *Institutiones,* I, n. 579; Toso, *Commentaria Minora,* V, 163; Fanfani, *De Iure Religiosorum,* n. 276; Prümmer, *Manuale,* p. 288; Canuto, "De regimine domus studiorum in religione clericali exempta ad normam can. 588," *Apollinaris,* IX (1936), 33, 34.

> fore the reception of Orders, cannot be appointed as the ordinary confessor of his charges, nor can he hear their confessions, unless according to the stipulation of canon 518, § 2.

It is evident, then, that the comon law has undergone a modification on this point. Nevertheless, the conclusion reached above in regard to the prefect of postulants remains valid. That is, this official is not forbidden by the common law to act as the confessor of the postulants. He is not mentioned by the *Sedes Sapientiae* when the spiritual prefect is spoken of, nor does the reason advanced for prohibiting the spiritual prefect from hearing his subjects' confessions have any application in the case of most postulants.

According to the writer's view, then, the prefect of postulants does not have any power in the external government of the community unless it is granted to him by special law. Consequently he is not forbidden by the canons of the Code, in consequence of the mind of the legislator, to hear, even habitually, the sacramental confessions of the postulants.

As was mentioned above, the prefect of postulants who has authority in the external government of the community should be considered as a superior rather than as the master of novices. Much, however, depends on the degree of authority vested in the prefect. If the latter exercises his authority with great dependence on the local superior, he seems to come under the enactments of canon 518, §§ 2, 3, inasmuch as he does not possess that independence which is proper to the master of novices.[68]

In each case it will be necessary, first, to decide whether the prefect of postulants proceeds after the manner of the local superior or after the manner of the master of novices. Having ascertained this, one may then apply the respective canons 518, §§ 2, 3 and 891. It is true that the legislator has not included in the Code any canon which decides the case under consideration by expressly mentioning the prefect of postulants by name. Nevertheless, he has furnished general principles in the light of which one may determine a norm of action in the cases not specifically provided for by

[68] Canon 561, § 1.

the law.[69] Consequently, when the prefect of postulants possesses authority in the external government of the community, he bears a marked resemblance to the superior and the master of novices inasmuch as all alike are endowed with external authority, although one may differ from the other in the degree of authority exercised. Since the prefect of postulants in the case under discussion possesses authority in the external forum, and since the policy of separation of the sacramental and the external forum is a principle of law, it follows that the reason which forbids the superior and the master of novices to hear the confessions of their subjects also prevails in the case of the prefect of postulants, and, consequently, the latter is bound by the same norms in his procedure.

Therefore, as far as the general law is concerned, postulants may habitually approach the master of novices or the prefect of postulants to make their confessions to them, unless the latter possess authority over the postulants in the external forum.

3. *Manifestation of Conscience*

Manifestation of conscience is described as the disclosure of one's state of mind and soul by revealing one's virtues, defects, temptations, trials, passions, difficulties, doubts, inclinations, and intentions in order that the person to whom the disclosure is made may acquire a satisfactory knowledge of one's spiritual condition and lead the way to one's spiritual perfection.[70]

The purpose of making the manifestation of conscience is to obtain help and direction from men experienced in leading souls to perfection. The good that is directly and immediately sought is the spiritual good of the individual, although the good of the institute may also be promoted indirectly and secondarily by way of improvement in the conduct of the religious.[71]

Canon 530, § 1, which treats of the manifestation of conscience, strictly forbids religious superiors to induce their subjects to mani-

[69] Canon 20.

[70] Vermeersch-Creusen, *Epitome*, I, n. 650; Larraona, "Commentarium Codicis," *CpR*, XII (1931), 128; Berutti, *Institutiones*, III, n. 55.

[71] Larraona, "art. cit.," *loc. cit.*

fest their consciences to them.[72] Postulants are included here for the simple reason that they are subjects of the religious superior, "*personae subiectae*" which term is used in this canon.[73]

The phrase "all religious superiors" ("*omnes religiosi Superiores*") embraces all those who according to the law are considered superiors, general, provincial, local, men and women. The term "superior" is to be taken in the strict sense, and is not to be extended to those who in a wide sense are called superiors, as for example, the assistant to the local superior.[74] Berutti asserts that the phrase "*omnes religiosi Superiores*" embraces every superior who from the common or the special law has dominative power by reason of his office. Thus he says that the master of novices and, under certain circumstances, the spiritual prefect are included under the law of canon 530, § 1, according to the wording of the law: the master of novices, because from the common law he is entrusted with the government of the novices, and the spiritual prefect, when according to the constitutions he is entrusted with the rule of the students in almost the same way as the master is entrusted with the rule of the novices.[75] It seems logical that he would also include here the prefect of postulants. His reason is based on the terminology of canon 530, § 1, which uses the words "*omnes religiosi Superiores . . . personas sibi subiectas.*" He points out that this wording is very broad and includes all kinds of superiors. Furthermore, he says, it mentions persons subject to the superiors, and not simply religious subjects to superiors.

[72] "Omnes religiosi Superiores districte vetantur personas sibi subiectas quoquo modo inducere ad conscientiae manifestationem sibi peragendam."

[73] Schaefer, *De Religiosis,* n. 689; Coronata, *Institutiones,* I, n. 557, nota (8); Goyeneche, *De Religiosis,* n. 33; Larraona, "Commentarium Codicis," *CpR,* XII (1931), 127; Voltas, "De Aperienda, Directionis Causa, Superioribus Conscientia," *CpR,* I (1920), 148. Vermeersch-Creusen in their seventh edition mention that they are correcting an opinion which they held in the third edition of their work, so that they now no longer believe that postulants are to be included among those from whom the superiors may not exact this manifestation.—*Epitome,* I. n. 650.

[74] Cf. Wernz-Vidal, *Ius Canonicum,* III, n. 213; Ferreres, *Institutiones,* I, n. 840; and the authors cited in the preceding footnote.

[75] *Institutiones,* III, n. 55.

It is the writer's opinion that the prefect of postulants does not fall under the prohibition enacted in canon 530, § 1. While most of the authors do not mention this fact expressly, it appears that it can be deduced from their exclusion of the master of novices and the spiritual prefect from the ambit of this canon. Even Berutti would not disagree if the sole consideration is the office of the prefect of postulants mentioned in the common law.

If by the constitutions the prefect of postulants is given some authority in the external forum, he may seek a manifestation of conscience from the postulants, provided that he uses persuasion and suggestion, and not force and fear. The reason for this view is based on the duty of the prefect of postulants who exercises an office different from that of the local superior. The prefect's duty is to form character in the souls of the postulants by means of their study of the Rules and constitutions, by means of prayer and meditation, and also of attention to those matters which pertain to the vows and virtues.[76]

Certainly the aim of the prefect of postulants can be better realized when a manifestation of conscience is made to him by his subjects. Vermeersch-Creusen[77] assert that such a manifestation on the part of novices is necessary for their proper training. It seems that the same reason can be applied here if the prefect of postulants has charge of the postulants in a similar manner. It must always be remembered, however, that the Code places no obligation on the postulants to reveal their innermost spiritual life.

In conclusion it may be said that even if the prefect of postulants has authority by special law in the external forum, he is permitted to urge in the manner of a kindly request or of a gracious invitation a manifestation of conscience from the postulants. By receiving this manifestation he becomes better able to aid them in their

---

[76] Gill (*The Spiritual Prefect in Clerical Religious Houses of Study,* The Catholic University of America Canon Law Studies, n. 216 [Washington, D. C.: The Catholic University of America Press, 1945], p. 102) holds this view in regard to the spiritual prefect and the professed subject to him. The present writer has adapted it to the prefect of postulants because of the similarity of the two offices.

[77] *Epitome,* I, n. 650.

doubts, difficulties, and temptations, which may endanger their vocation. The postulants, however, have no obligation to accede to his request, and the prefect of postulants may not change his attitude toward those who seek assistance from others.[78]

E. Burial of the Postulants

Ecclesiastical burial consists in the bringing of the body to the church, in the performance of the obsequies there, and in the final transporting of the body to the place of interment.[79] The faithful are ordinarily taken for burial to their own parish church, unless the deceased had legitimately chosen another church;[80] but professed religious and also novices are buried from the church or the oratory of the religious house, or at least from a church or an oratory of the religious institute.[81] Novices, however, still retain the right to choose another church. In all cases wherein a subject of the religious superior, even a novice, is concerned, both the right of saying the liturgical prayers when the body is removed from the place of death, and the right of transporting the body to the church of burial, always belong to the religious superior.[82] Servants who were actually in the service of the religious and who lived habitually within the religious house may also be buried from the church or the oratory of the religious house, if they die in the religious house.[83] According to an official interpretation of the Pontifical Commission, postulants and apostolic students do not enjoy the right given to the professed, to the novices and to the servants mentioned in canon 1221, even though such postulants and students were cared for in their last illness by the local religious superior, as provided for in canon 514, §1,[84] nor do others who have resided there as guests, students, or patients.[85] If, how-

[78] Gill, *The Spiritual Prefect in Religious Houses of Study,* p. 102.

[79] Cf. canons 1204 and 1215.

[80] Cf. canons 1216 and 1223.

[81] Canon 1221, § 1.

[82] Cf. canon 1221, § 1; Coronata, *Institutiones,* II (4. ed., 1951), n. 805, 3° (e).

[83] Cf. canon 1221, § 3.

[84] PCI, 20 iul. 1929—*AAS,* XXI (1929), 573.

[85] Cf. canon 1222.

ever, the postulant, the apostolic student, or the servant who died outside the religious house had before his death lawfully chosen to be buried from the church of the religious, he would be permitted burial from the religious church, as would anyone of the faithful who had chosen such a church for his burial.[86]

In regard to the burial of his own subjects, i.e., the professed, the novices, and the servants mentioned in canon 1221, § 3, the local superior in clerical exempt institutes has the right to say the liturgical prayers when the body is removed from the place of death (*ius levandi*), to accompany it to the religious church or oratory (*ius deducendi*), to conduct the funeral services in the church (*ius exsequia celebrandi*), and to transport the body to the grave (*ius comitandi*). These rights do not extend to the burial of the postulants or apostolic students,[87] but they belong to the local superior even if the religious does not die within the religious house, as long as the superior provides for the transportation of the body to the church or the oratory of the religious house.[88] In regard to the burial of postulants, of servants who die outside the religious house, and of apostolic students, the local superior has the right of conducting the funeral services in the church and of accompanying the body to the grave if these persons have chosen to be buried from the church or the oratory of the religious. The competent pastor, however, must be granted the *ius levandi* and the *ius deducendi*.[89]

In short, then, the funerals of postulants and apostolic students is regulated in all cases by the norms of canons 1216-1218, that is to say, by the general norms that regulate the burial of the faithful.

F. *Profession in Articulo Mortis*

The privilege of profession *in articulo mortis* was first granted by St. Pius V (1566-1572) to nun novices of the Dominican

[86] Canons 1223, § 1, 1225; Coronata, *Institutiones*, II, n. 800, (c).
[87] Canons 1204 and 1231, § 2.
[88] Canons 1221, § 2, and 1218, § 3.
[89] Canon 1230, § 3.

Order.[90] Prior to this concession such a privilege does not seem to have been mentioned by canonists. It appears St. Pius V originated both the idea and the privilege to be granted *in articulo mortis.*[91] Most of the authors held that this privilege was enjoyed by novices of both sexes of any religious institute which shared in this privilege of the Dominican Order.[92] Not all authors, however, admitted this.[93] Piatus Montensis (J. J. Loiseaux, 1815-1904) cited[94] Dominicus Ursaya (fl. 1730-1736) and Bartholomaeus de Vecchis (Bartholomaeus a S. Fausto, 1571-1636) as holding that the privilege granted by St. Pius V was abrogated by reason of the Constitution *In tanta* of Gregory XIII (1572-1585),[95] and the Constitution *Romanus Pontifex* of Paul V (1605-1621).[96] Nevertheless, it appears that St. Pius V's Constitution continued in force. Gregory XIII did not revoke all the acts of Pius V granted in favor of regulars, but he revoked only those which he himself expressly designated. The Constitution *Summi Sacerdotii,* by means of which St. Pius V granted the privilege of profession *in articulo mortis,* was not mentioned among those of his Constitutions which Gregory XIII revoked. Nor was this Constitution revoked by Paul V. His Constitution, it is true, revoked all indul-

---

90 Const. *Summi Sacerdotii,* 23 aug. 1570—*Bullarum Diplomatum et Privilegiorum Sanctorum Romanorum Pontificum* (Taurinensis editio, 25 vols., Augustae Taurinorum, 1857-1872), VII, 849-851. For a historical summary of this privilege cf. Hofmeister, "*Professio religiosa in articulo mortis* unter dem neuen Recht," *Linzer-theologisch-praktische Quartalschrift,* LXXIV (1921), 493-500.

91 *Analecta Ecclesiastica* (Romae, 1893-1911), II (1894), 498; De Langogne, "De la profession religieuse anticipée *in articulo mortis,*" *Le Canoniste Contemporain* (Paris, 1878-1922), XVIII (1895), 2.

92 Cf., e.g., Schmalzgrueber, *Ius Ecclesiasticum Universum,* Lib. III, tit. XXXI, n. 48; Reiffenstuel, *Jus Canonicum Universum,* Lib. III, tit. XXXI, nn. 182, 183; Wernz-Vidal, *Ius Canonicum,* III, n. 296.

93 Cf. *Le Canoniste Contemporain,* XVIII (1895), 3.

94 *Praelectiones Juris Regularis* (3. ed., 2 vols., Tornaci, 1906), I, 101, 102.

95 § 6—*Bull. Rom.,* VIII, 39. This constitution was issued on March 1, 1573.

96 §§ 8, 19—*Bull. Rom.,* XI, 318. This constitution was issued on May 23, 1606.

gences granted to regulars, and clearly stated which ones the Pope from that time on granted them. It is likewise true that certain indulgences were connected with the act of profession *in articulo mortis*. Yet the majority of the authors continued to maintain that the privilege itself had not been recalled by this act of Paul V.[97]

In order to remove all doubt in this matter and to settle any dispute as to which religious groups enjoyed this privilege, St. Pius X issued the decree *Spirituali consolationi.*[98] In it he extended this privilege to all orders, congregations and societies, and likewise to the institutes which follow the common life without vows. This decree settled not only the dispute as to which religious groups enjoyed this privilege, but also the question that had been raised by some authors, namely whether or not the original grant of St. Pius V had ever been recalled. In this decree it was stated that the privilege was already enjoyed by those religious institutes which shared in the privileges of the Dominican Order. It was likewise stated that some other institutes had obtained the privilege by special grant from the Holy See, or had incorporated it into their constitutions, which in turn had received the approval of the Holy See.[99]

Concern arose again regarding the existence of this privilege when it was noted that nowhere in the Code was profession *in articulo mortis* mentioned.[100] The reasons for the concern were the following: 1) The decree *Spirituali consolationi* of St. Pius X had changed the nature of the concession from that of a privilege to that of a general law. Hence, as a general law, since it was neither explicitly or implicitly mentioned in the Code, it had lost all its force according to the principles of canon 6, 6°; 2) This privilege moreover seemed useless after the enactment of the Code, since canon 567, § 1, stated that novices shared in all the spiritual privileges granted to the institute in which they were novices. Thus, in the case of death a novice would receive exactly the same

[97] Piatus, *Praelectiones Juris Regularis,* I, 102.

[98] S. C. de Religiosis, decr. *Spirituali consolationi,* 10 sept. 1912—*AAS,* IV (1912), 589-590.

[99] Decr. *Spirituali consolationi*—*AAS,* IV (1912), 589.

[100] Cf. canon 567.

suffrages as would a deceased religious who had made religious profession.[101]

Most of the authors,[102] however, argued that it was not at all clear or certain that the legal character of the grant had been changed. Rather, the privilege had simply been made universal by the decree of St. Pius X and had thus become a general privilege, not a general law. Nor was the concession made useless simply because novices were entitled to the same suffrages as were the professed religious should they be overtaken by death. A profession of vows pronounced on one's deathbed had the effect of spiritually consoling the dying novice, and furthermore gained him the graces and supernatural merit attached to this act of religious profession.

The writer believes that this opinion was the better one juridically. But at any rate the discussion is now mainly a matter of historical interest. The Holy See in 1922 settled the dispute by declaring that the decree *Spirituali consolationi* was still in effect, and at the same time it took occasion to specify the conditions for the effects of profession *in articulo mortis.*[103] Of practical import to this study is the question whether or not postulants too may enjoy this privilege. The title used in the decree *Spirituali consolationi* and in that of 1922 reads: "*De professione religiosa in articulo mortis novitiis vel postulantibus permissa.*"[104] Commentators noticed this immediately, and some maintained that this privilege could be extended to dying postulants as well as to novices.[105] Others, however, maintained that only in the title of this decree were postulants mentioned, and, that the body of the

---

[101] Goyeneche, "Consultationes," *CpR,* I (1920), 51-52; "Annotationes," *CpR,* IV (1923), 260-261.

[102] Cf. Goyeneche, "Annotationes," *CpR,* IV (1923), 261. where in note 4 he enumerated a number of authors who held this view.

[103] S. C. de Religiosis, decr. 30 dec. 1922—*AAS,* XV (1923), 156-158.

[104] Decr. *Spirituali consolationi—AAS,* IV (1912), 589; decr. 30 dec. 1922—*AAS,* XV (1923), 156.

[105] Vermeersch, "De professione novitii vel probandi in articulo mortis," *Periodica,* XII (1923), (159)-(162); Maroto, "Annotationes," *CpR,* X (1929), 338.

declaration did not mention the postulants at all, but throughout referred to novices and the novitiate, probationers and probation (*probandi, probandatus*).[106] This decree of 1922, just as the decree of 1912, in section one, restricted this privilege to those who had already begun their novitiate or probation, and this limitation would have been meaningless, if the privilege had applied to postulants. Although the intrinsic arguments given for the view of this latter group of authors seemed to discount the contentions of the other commentators, Goyeneche[107] nevertheless admitted that postulants could be admitted to this deathbed profession of vows. He based his conclusion on a statement of Vermeersch, namely that it was the mind of the Sacred Congregation to extend this privilege to postulants.[108] This alleged intention seems to have been untrue, for Vermeersch ultimately changed his opinion and expressly taught the opposite, that is to say, that postulants are excluded from the use of this privilege.[109] Goyeneche then reverted to his original opinion, mentioning that it was the practice of the Sacred Congregation in approving sets of new constitutions to delete from them any reference which suggests that postulants enjoy the privilege of profession *in articulo mortis*.[110]

In conclusion, then, it may be stated that postulants are not included within the scope of the privilege of deathbed profession. The more liberal view has little intrinsic probability, since it rests chiefly on the use of the word postulants ("*postulantibus*") in the title of the decree of 1922. Its extrinsic probability loses almost

---

[106] The terms *probandus* and *probandatus* are frequently employed in societies living in common without vows as the equivalents of novice and novitiate in religious institutes. Cf. W. A. Stanton, *De Societatibus sive Virorum sive Mulierum in Communi Viventium sine Votis* (2. ed., Halifax: Major Seminary of the Sacred Heart of Mary, 1936), pp. 128-135; Goyeneche, "Annotationes," *CpR*, IV (1923), 262; "Consultationes," *CpR*, V (1924), 165-166; Anon., "Dying Postulants Cannot be Admitted to Profession," *The American Ecclesiastical Review* (Philadelphia, 1889-1943; Washington, D. C., 1944 —), C (1939), 447-452.

[107] "Consultationes," *CpR*, V (1924), 166.

[108] *Periodica*, XII (1923), (161).

[109] Vermeersch-Creusen, *Epitome*, I, n. 720.

[110] "Consultationes," *CpR*, XIII (1932), 39-40.

all its weight when it is borne in mind that the authors who still hold it base their view, at least to a great extent, upon authors who have, for better reasons, given up the position they had previously taken.[111] One final argument may be drawn from a reply given by the Sacred Congregation of Religious and cited by Bastien (1866-1940).[112] This reply, according to Bastien, was given on March 28, 1925, and was confirmed by Pope Pius XI on April 5 of that same year. According to it postulants could not be included among those for whom the privilege of profession in danger of death had been granted. This reply of the Sacred Congregation, however, did not appear in the *Acta Apostolicae Sedis*, nor, to the knowledge of the writer, has it ever been published officially elsewhere.

---

[111] Coronata (*Institutiones,* I, n. 587), for example, follows Vermeersch in his earlier opinion and extends this privilege to postulants, although the latter had already taken the opposite view.

[112] *Directoire Canonique* (4. ed., 1933), p. 332.

CHAPTER XI

FULFILLMENT OR DISCHARGE OF THE CANONICAL POSTULANCY

A. Retreat and General Confession

Since no juridical bond exists between the institute and the postulant, the latter is free to leave at any time and the competent superior is free to dismiss the postulant whenever a just cause for such a dismissal arises. If the postulant perseveres in the institute then by force of the common law there is not required any special examination other than that which is demanded for women postulants before their entrance into the novitiate.[1] The constitutions, however, must be observed on this point.[2]

The Code in canon 541 merely states:

> *Postulantes, antequam novitiatum incipiant, exercitiis spiritualibus vacent per octo saltem integros dies; et, iuxta prudens confessarii iudicium, praemittant generalem anteactae vitae confessionem.*

No reference in the Code indicates the origin of this law. It seems, however, to have come from numbers 77 and 78 of the 1901 *Normae* and from the provision found in § 6 of the papal Constitution *Cum ad regularem* of Clement VIII.[3] The first of these numbers ordered that candidates before beginning their novitiate by taking the habit, were to make a retreat of ten days,[4] and the second prescribed that, in accordance with the counsel of their confessor, they were to make a general confession of their past

[1] Cf. canon 552; *supra*, p. 121-122.

[2] Schaefer, *De Religiosis*, n. 777.

[3] Constitutio *Cum ad regularem*, 19 mart. 1603—*Fontes*, n. 189.

[4] *Normae*, n. 77: "Candidatae antequam per habitus receptionem novitiatum incipiant, exercitia spiritualia peragant per decem dies."

lives.[5] The earlier papal Constitution had ordered that novices at the very outset of their novitiate were to make a general confession of their whole life.[6] It may be asked whether the prescription of canon 541 regarding the spiritual exercises applies to all aspirants to the novitiate, so that it applies even when the text of the institute's constitutions warrants the omission of the postulancy?

The answers to these questions are rather clear from a comparison of canon 541 with canon 539, § 1. The subject of canon 541 is "*Postulantes,*" and the entire content of the canon is addressed to postulants. Hence, the time to be spent in the discharge of the spiritual exercises, as well as the making of a general confession, is a provision that applies to those who are actually bound to the postulancy. Canon 539, § 1, indicates who these persons are. In the case, therefore, of clerics or of teaching brothers, even when they are to profess perpetual vows, or in the case of religious with temporary vows who are not obliged to the postulancy by their constitutions, none of the enactments of the Code in regard to the postulancy have application or force.[7]

On the other hand, if one classifies an aspirant to the religious life as a postulant by reason of the common law or of the special law of the institute, the canons on the postulancy must be observed. Consequently, canon 541, which requires eight full days for the spiritual retreat, will have to be complied with, unless the Holy See has approved a curtailment of this retreat in the special law of an institute.[8]

Constitutions, sometimes, require that candidates for the novitiate discharge the spiritual exercises for eight days prior to their admission, as mentioned by the common law, without any refer-

---

[5] *Normae,* n. 78: "Praemittant etiam, iuxta prudens iudicium confessarii, generalem anteactae vitae confessionem."

[6] Const. *Cum ad regularem,* 19 mart. 1603, § 6: "Statim atque novitii ad habitum recepti et in locum novitiatus introducti fuerint, per generalem omnium peccatorum confessionem, totius anteactae vitae conscientiam discutiant et expurgent."—*Fontes,* n. 189.

[7] Berutti, *Institutiones,* III, n. 65; Fanfani, *De Iure Religiosorum,* n. 189.

[8] Balzer, *The Computation of Time in a Canonical Novitiate,* p. 85.

ence to a postulancy at all. Since these exercises are made prior to the beginning of the novitiate, and cannot be counted as part of the year of the novitiate, they equivalently imply a postulancy of eight days based on the special law of the institute.[9]

These spiritual exercises are to be performed before the postulants are admitted to the novitiate, and, if it is a case of women postulants, only after the prescribed examination of canon 552 has been completed by the bishop or his delegate. This law does not necessarily require that the last day of the retreat coincide with the day of investiture with the habit. Although this would perhaps

---

[9] Cf., e.g., *Constitutions of the Society of St. Joseph of the Sacred Heart* (Vatican Polyglot Press, 1932), n. 56. Larraona mentions that only postulants, that is, only those for whom a true canonical postulancy is of obligation, are held to the requirement of this canon by the rigor of the law. In general practice, however, the retreat will be obligatory for all those who are preparing to enter a novitiate, since the Sacred Congregation of Religious is accustomed to insert a requirement calling for such a retreat in nearly all constitutions, when they are submitted for its approval.—"Commentarium Codicis," *CpRM*, XVI (1935), 378. There, in note (104), he cites the following institutes as examples of those which demand a retreat of all candidates according to the norms of canon 541 before they are admitted to the novitiate: The Camaldulese Congregation of Monte Corno (1934), n. 238; the Hermits of St. Augustine (1926), n. 206; the Cistercians of the Strict Observance (1925), n. 146; the Dominicans (1932), n. 92; the Discalced Carmelites (1928), n. 237; the Brothers of St. John of God (1907), n. 43; the Friars Minor Conventual (1932), n. 93; the Friars Minor (1922), n. 38; the Friars Minor Capuchin (1926), p. 37 (10)-38; the Priests of the Blessed Sacrament (1923), n. 343 (10 days); the Priests of the Sacred Heart (1923), n. 28.

Nevertheless, there are constitutions in which this precept of a retreat is omitted altogether, or only an indefinite number of days is ordered, or there is granted the faculty for dispensing from the prescribed number of days. Cf., e.g., *the Constitutions of the Oblates of Mary Immaculate* (1928), n. 693; and *the Constitutions of the Society of the Divine Word* (1922), n. 39. In the latter there occurs the following directive: "Admissi ad novitiatum, ante susceptionem habitus, exercitiis spiritualibus vacent per octo integros dies, et iuxta prudens confessarii iudicium praemittant generalem anteactae vitae confessionem, nisi forte pro clericis consultius videatur post quatuor dierum exercitia habitum concedere, maioribus exercitiis ad mensem fere delatis ut interim primis vitae spiritualis rudimentis imbuti, mense elapso, potiore cum fructu, per octo dies exerceantur."

be the better arrangement, it is not forbidden that a few days intervene between the retreat and the entrance into the novitiate.[10]

Although the law is silent in regard to the number and the nature of the spiritual exercises, they should constitute a real retreat. This is evident from the fact that the same words are used by the Code in designation of the retreats imposed on candidates for Holy Orders (canon 1001), on priests (canon 126), and on religious (canon 595, § 1). Both the dictates of custom and the text of the pontifical documents on the spiritual exercises suppose that the retreatant will put aside all other occupations to devote himself during some days to the exercises of the retreat (mental prayer, examination of conscience, spiritual reading, etc.).[11]

As was seen above, the 1901 *Normae* required that ten days be spent in these exercises. They did not, however, specify that these ten days had to be integral, and therefore one could count among them both the day the retreat started and the one on which it finished, although the retreat was commenced in the evening of the first day and was brought to a close in the morning of the tenth day.

This custom may still be followed, and indeed it is quite frequently retained by the constitutions of the various institutes. The law requires at least eight integral or complete days, and thus the way is open for the constitutions to demand that a longer period than this be spent in retreat prior to the reception of the habit.[12]

Since the time for the exercises does not have an explicitly or implicitly assigned starting point, the natural, rather than the civil reckoning of time is to be employed.[13] This means that the norm is taken from canon 34, § 2, and that the time is reckoned

[10] Larraona, "Commentarium Codicis," *CpRM,* XVI (1935), 379; Schaefer, *De Religiosis,* n. 777.

[11] Creusen, *Religious in the Code,* n. 175; Larraona, "Commentarium Codicis," *CpRM,* XVI (1935), 379.

[12] Larraona, "Commentarium Codicis," *CpRM,* XVI (1935), 380.

[13] Dubé, *The General Principles for the Reckoning of Time in Canon Law,* The Catholic University of America Canon Law Studies, n. 144 (Washington, D.C.: The Catholic University of America Press, 1941), pp. 205, 216, 217.

from moment to moment (*"de momento ad momentum"*). The time is continuous, as canon 541 clearly implies[14] and, therefore, if the retreat began at ten o'clock in the morning of the 15th, it would end at the same hour in the morning of the 23rd, on the assumption, of course, that in this case the minimum duration of eight days was called for.

If the reception into the novitiate should be delayed by reason of sickness or of some other just cause, the provision of canon 1001, § 2, relative to the repetition of the spiritual exercises should be applied.[15] If the delay extends beyond six months, the retreat must be repeated; if the delay is less than six months, the ordinary should be consulted and his decision observed.[16]

The wisdom of the second requirement of canon 541, namely, the making of a general confession, should be apparent to all. There is no better or more solid foundation on which to build the religious life than upon an earnest and sincere purification of the heart. Since this pertains to the internal forum, the law requires that in each case the confessor weigh the necessity, utility and advisability of such a confession before any strict obligation will arise for the postulant. The confessor here referred to should obviously be the one whom the postulant has chosen and to whom he has gone during the course of the postulancy. It appears that the confessor should not lightly dispense from this provision of the common law, but that he should rather define its limits and instruct the postulant as to the best manner of complying with it.

B. Termination of the Postulancy

The postulancy is brought to a natural conclusion upon the postulant's admission into the novitiate, for which the postulant was preparing himself throughout the days of the retreat. But it may also be terminated through outside intervention, either through

[14] "Postulantes, antequam novitiatum incipiant, exercitiis spiritualibus vacent per octo saltem dies. . . ."

[15] Beste, *Introductio in Codicem,* at canon 541; Tabera, *Derecho de Los Religiosos* (Madrid: Editorial Coculsa, 1948), p. 216.

[16] Schaefer, *De Religiosis,* n. 777, with note (72).

the dismissal of the postulant by the proper superior, or through the postulant's voluntary withdrawal from the institute.

Those superiors, as a general rule, to whom it pertains to admit candidates to the postulancy may also without any juridical formality dismiss them. The Code has nothing to say about the manner of their dismissal, and rightly so, for, since there is no juridical bond existing between the postulant and the religious institute, his dismissal should not be considered as a juridical matter. *A fortiori* one should apply to this dismissal what canon 571 prescribes for the dismissal of novices, namely, that the superior is not bound to reveal to the postulant the reason for his dismissal.

Even after such a dismissal or withdrawal from the institute, the former postulant may be re-admitted to the same or a different religious institute. If he enters another institute, he must furnish testimonial letters from the major superior of the institute in which he was a postulant.

The special provisions for the extern sisters in monasteries of cloistered nuns contain a verbatim repetition of these two requirements of canon 541 as applicable to these extern sisters.[17]

C. Time Intervening Between Postulancy and Novitiate

The writer would not hesitate to sanction a few days' absence from the monastery, for example, for the sake of visiting one's parents, after the postulancy is completed and before the beginning of the novitiate. The mind, however, of the legislator seems to be that a suitable candidate, once he has completed the postulancy, should begin the novitiate at once, but that this does not rule out a few days' deferment. It is sufficient that a moral union exists between the postulancy and the novitiate.[18]

Most of the authors substantially agree on this point. They likewise agree in making an exception when postulants in monasteries of nuns are concerned.[19] Schaefer felt it allowable for the postulant

[17] S.C. de Religiosis, Statuta a sororibus externis monasteriorum monialium cuiusque ordinis servanda, 16 iul. 1931, n. 24—*Apollinaris,* IV (1931), 348.

[18] Cappello, *Summa,* II, 34, 6.

[19] Schaefer, *De Religiosis,* n. 777; Berutti, *Institutiones,* III, n. 67;

to visit his home before commencing the novitiate if the constitutions and approved customs of the institute permitted such a visit.[20] Coronata recognizes the licitness of such visits for those who are not subject to the cloister of nuns, but adds immediately that it would be more in accord with the spirit of the law if the novitiate began at the close of the postulancy.[21] It goes without saying that such visits, even when allowed, should be brief, lest there be a violation of the canon which requires that the spiritual exercises at the end of the postulancy should precede immediately, at least morally so, the admission to the novitiate.[22]

A postulant in a monastery of nuns may not leave the enclosure before commencing the novitiate. Canon 540, § 3, makes it clear that such a postulant is bound by the law of the cloister. This provision, as it is expressed in the common law, pertains to the time of the actual postulancy. The Instruction *Intera cetera* (n. 19) of the Sacred Congregation of Religious of March 25, 1956, makes it clear that postulants may not leave the cloister after the postulancy is completed.[23]

Schaefer was of the opinion that in those cases in which the postulant is allowed to visit his home before he is admitted to the novitiate the spiritual retreat should be made after his return from such a visit. That is to say, the retreat should immediately precede his entrance into the novitiate.[24] None of the other authors whom the writer consulted seem to mention this. While in practice this may be the more acceptable mode of procedure, it does not appear that such an arrangement can be urged as being of necessity.

Fanfani directly proposed a further question. It involved the interval between the postulancy and the novitiate when the candidate remains in the postulancy apart from any prolongation of it

---

Coronata, *Institutiones,* I, n. 566; Vermeersch-Creusen, *Epitome,* I, n. 668. Cf. S. C. de Religiosis, instr. 25 mart. 1956—*AAS,* XLVIII (1956), 512-526.

[20] Schaefer, *loc. cit.*

[21] *Institutiones,* I, n. 566.

[22] Cappello, *Summa,* II, 34, 7.

[23] Cf. also Reply of S. C. de Religiosis, 7 nov. 1916—*AAS,* VII (1916), 446; *Periodica,* VIII (1919), 227.

[24] *De Religiosis,* n. 777.

by the superior, and thus responded to the correlative *dubium* about the immediate inception of the novitiate. He pointed out that, although canon 539, § 1, ordains that the postulants are to make a postulancy before they are admitted to the novitiate ("*antequam ad novitiatum admittantur*"), the common law does not say that the postulancy must be made immediately ("*immediate*") before the novitiate. Therefore, he continued, nothing prevents the postulant from remaining as a candidate for the novitiate without at once ("*statim*") entering upon the novitiate. He immediately warned, however, that "at once" ("*statim*") implies that the beginning of the novitiate can not be deferred for long, for to do so would be contrary to common usage and the mind of the legislator, unless the constitutions duly approved after the promulgation of the Code would expressly permit it.[25]

---

[25] *De Iure Religiosorum,* n. 189, Dubium I.

CONCLUSIONS

A brief recapitulation of the principal conclusions reached in the foregoing study may here be indicated as follows:

1. An initial period of probation, which may be considered as a foreshadowing of the present institute of the postulancy, is as old as the organized forms of religious life itself. But this period of probation was not a requirement in all of the ancient religious institutes.

2. The duration of this period in the first centuries of monasticism was not rigidly determined; accordingly, much was left to the prudence and discretion of superiors in individual cases.

3. Although some elasticity continued to exist, it was almost a universal custom by the eleventh century in the Western Church for all candidates for the religious life to undergo some form of initial probation, comparable to the postulancy. This period, due to the influence of the Rule of St. Benedict, was generally rather short, and still remained completely dispensable at the judgment of the superior.

4. Special law requiring a postulancy for lay brothers dates back as far as the beginning of the *conversi* institute itself.

5. No general legislation existed in relation to the postulancy before January 1, 1911.

6. For male lay religious, even though they pronounce perpetual vows, there is no previous requirement of a postulancy as long as they belong to a category of religious other than lay brothers (*conversi*).

7. The postulancy need not be undertaken by a lay brother who has had some previous probation as a clerical novice in the same institute, nor need it be repeated by a religious who, for some reason, has been forced to interrupt his novitiate through his absence from the novitiate house beyond thirty days, nor by one who, after leaving the religious state during the novitiate, upon a brief absence repents of his decision and returns to the religious house. The same is true in the case of a secularized religious who in virtue of an apostolic indult is re-admitted into his religious institute.

8. The *minimum* length of the common law postulancy is six months, which may be extended, but not shortened by the constitutions. The time requirement for the postulancy in institutes whose members are professed with temporary vows is left entirely to the constitutions.

9. The major superior may prolong the original term of the postulancy as it is prescribed by either the special or the common law regardless of how long the basic term of the postulancy may be.

10. The word "*peragant*" of canon 539, § 1, is of precept only, and hence the postulancy which the common law demands is never required for a valid entrance into the novitiate.

11. The period of the postulancy must be computed according to the rule established in canon 34, § 3, 3°. The time need not be absolutely continuous, and hence only a moral continuity is required.

12. The major superior may shorten the postulancy by a few days whenever a just and reasonable cause exists.

13. The postulancy may be made in the novitiate house or in any other house of the institute in which the regular discipline is carefully observed. Prudence dictates that the preferable place for the postulancy is the novitiate house.

14. While the separation of the postulants from the novices cannot be urged as a strict requirement, at least the lay postulants who live with the lay novices should be separated from the choir novices and postulants. There must always be placed over the postulants a prefect, concerning whose qualifications the constitutions will have to be followed.

15. The wearing of a habit or at least of a distinctive uniform dress cannot be urged as a common law obligation for the postulants. Their garb need only be modest in all respects and different from that of the novices.

16. Postulants in monasteries of nuns are bound by the law of the cloister, but they do not incur the excommunication reserved for nuns who leave the cloister unlawfully.

17. The competent superior for the admission of the postulants is the major superior.

18. Only those listed impediments of canon 542 which are

more accurate determinations of canon 538, or from which by their very nature or from the practice of the Church usually no dispensation is given, may be extended to the postulancy. The superior is not obliged to be in possession of the testimonial letters mentioned in canon 544 before he admits a candidate to the postulancy.

19. The postulancy begins juridically when the candidate takes up residence in the religious house with the permission of the competent superior.

20. Nun postulants are bound by the law of dowry. All postulants must pay what the constitutions prescribe for food and clothing during the postulancy, or whatever an explicit agreement has determined on the same basis at the beginning of the postulancy.

21. Postulants may perform some of the external works of the institute and also may engage in study. During the postulancy they are subject to the various superiors of the institute by virtue of a pact or in consequence of an implied contract.

22. Women postulants must be examined with reference to their full knowledge of and complete liberty for their action. This examination is to be made by the local ordinary or by his delegate before the postulants may be admitted to the novitiate.

23. Postulants need not attend the bi-weekly instructions in Christian doctrine prescribed in canon 509, but they should be present at the pious exhortations required in this same canon. Postulants in all lay religious institutes must, according to a decree of the Sacred Congregation of Religious, be diligently instructed in Christian doctrine. It seems that the pre-Code decree *Sacrosancta* demands the same for the *conversi* postulants in clerical institutes.

24. The local superior in clerical institutes has the right to administer Viaticum and extreme unction to the postulants ill within the religious house, but not when they are ill outside the house, unless he obtains the permission of the pastor of the place. In the case of nun postulants and postulants in lay institutes this right belongs to the ordinary confessor and the local pastor respectively when these postulants are ill within the religious house. Outside the house the local pastor alone is competent.

25. Postulants do not enjoy a share in the privileges and

favors of the religious institute, nor do they enjoy the common privileges of clerics. The privilege of profession *in articulo mortis* may not be extended to them.

26. Postulants are completely free in their choice of a confessor. The clerical superior, however, may not habitually hear their confessions. But is seems that postulants may, as far as the general law is concerned, even habitually confess to the clerical master of novices, or also to the clerical prefect of postulants, whenever these clerics possess the needed confessional jurisdiction, unless they possess authority over the postulants in the external forum.

27. Superiors are forbidden to induce postulants to make a manifestation of conscience to them. The master of novices and the prefect of postulants are bound by the spirit of this law rather than strictly by its letter.

28. The burial of postulants and apostolic students is ruled by the norms of canons 1216-1218.

29. Anyone classed as a postulant, whether by the special or by the common law, must observe the provisions of canon 541, with regard to the spiritual retreat and the general confession.

30. It is sufficient that a moral union exist between the postulancy and the novitiate.

31. The postulancy is naturally terminated by admission into the novitiate. It may also be terminated by the proper superior's dismissal of the postulant or by the latter's voluntary withdrawal from the religious institute.

BIBLIOGRAPHY

Sources

Acta Apostolicae Sedis, Commentarium Officiale, Romae, 1909—

Acta Sanctae Sedis, 41 vols., Romae, 1865-1908.

Bouscaren, T. L., *The Canon Law Digest,* 3 vols. with supplement through 1956, Milwaukee: Bruce, 1934—

Bullarum Diplomatum et Privilegiorum Sanctorum Romanorum Pontificum, Taurinensis Editio, 25 vols., Augustae Taurinorum, 1857-1872.

Caeremoniale Ordinis Recollectorum Sancti Augustini, Romae, 1950.

Codex Iuris Canonici Pii X Pontificis Maximi iussu digestus Benedicti Papae XV auctoritate promulgatus, ed. Petri Card. Gasparri, Romae: Typis Polyglottis Vaticanis, 1917.

Codex Regularum et Constitutionum Congregationis SS. Redemptoris.

Codicis Iuris Canonici Fontes, cura Emi Petri Card. Gasparri editi, 9 vols., Romae (postea Civitate Vaticana): Typis Polyglottis Vaticanis, 1923-1939. (Vols. VII-IX ed. cura et studio Emi Iustiniani Card. Serédi).

Collectanea in usum Secretariae Sacrae Congregationis Episcoporum et Regularium, ed. A. Bizzarri, Romae, 1885.

Constitutiones Ordinis Hospitalarii S. Joannis de Deo, Romae, 1927.

Constitutiones Ordinis Recollectorum Sancti Augustini, Romae, 1937.

Constitutiones Religionis Clericorum Regularium Pauperum Matris Dei Scholarum Piarum.

Constitutions of the Congregation of the Sisters of Notre Dame, 1937.

Constitutions of the Missionary Servants of the Most Blessed Trinity, Philadelphia, 1933.

Constitutions of the Oblates of Saint Francis de Sales, Childs, Maryland, 1927.

Constitutions of the Sisters of the Visitation after the Original Manuscripts, London: Manresa Press, 1930.

Constitutions of the Society of Mary, Dayton, Ohio, 1937.

Constitutions of the Society of St. Joseph of the Sacred Heart, Vatican: Polyglot Press, 1932.

Corpus Scriptorum Ecclesiasticorum Latinorum, editum consilio et impensis Academiae Litterarum Caesareae Vindobonensis, Vindobonae, 1866—

Guignard, Philippe, *Les monuments primitifs de la Règle Cisterciénne publiés d'après les manuscrits de l'Abbaye de Cîteaux,* Analecta Divionensia, X, Dijon, 1878.

Mansi, Ioannes, *Sacrorum Conciliorum Nova et Amplissima Collectio*. 53 vols. in 60. Paris-Leipzig-Arnhem, 1901-1927.

Migne, J. P. *Patrologiae Cursus Completus, Series Graeca*, 161 vols., Parisiis, 1857-1866.

———, *Patrologiae Cursus Completus, Series Latina*, 221 vols., Parisiis, 1844-1855.

Monumenta Germaniae Historica, Inde ab anno Christi quingentesimo usque ad annum millesimum et quingentesimum edidit Societas Aperiendis Fontibus Rerum Germanicarum Medii Aevi, *Legum Sectio* III, *Concilia*, I, *Concilia Aevi Merovingici*, ed. F. Maassen, Hannoverae 1893; *Concilia*, II, *Concilia Aevi Karolini*, Pars I, ed. A. Werminghoff, Hannoverae et Lipsiae, 1906.

Normae Secundum Quas S. Congregatio Episcoporum et Regularium procedere solet in Approbandis Novis Institutis Votorum Simplicium, Romae: Typis S.C. de Propaganda Fide, 1901.

Pallottini, Salvator, *Collectio Omnium Conclusionum et Resolutionum quae in causis propositis apud Sacram Congregationem Cardinalium S. Concilii Tridentini Interpretum prodierunt ab eius institutione, anno MDLXXIX ad MDCCCLX, distinctis titulis alphabetico ordine per materias digestas*, 18 vols., Romae, 1868-1893.

Rules and Constitutions of the Congregation of the Most Holy Cross and Passion of Our Lord Jesus Christ, Union City: The Sign Press, ca. 1931.

Statuta a sororibus externis monasteriorum monialium cuiusque ordinis servanda—Apollinaris, IV (1931), 345-361.

Reference Works

Allies, Thomas, *The Monastic Life*, London, 1896.

Augustine, Charles, *A Commentary on the New Code of Canon Law*, 8 vols., Vol. III, 5. ed., St. Louis: Herder, 1938.

Ayrinhac, H., *Penal Legislation in the New Code of Canon Law*, New York: Benziger Bros., 1936.

Bakalarcyzk, R., *De Novitiatu*, The Catholic University of America Canon Law Studies, n. 36, Washington, D. C.: The Catholic University of America, 1927.

Balzer, Ralph, *The Computation of Time in a Canonical Novitiate*, The Catholic University of America Canon Law Studies, n. 212, Washington, D. C.: The Catholic University of America Press, 1945.

Bastien, P., *Directoire Canonique a l'Usage des Congrégations à Voeux Simples*, 3. ed., Bruges: Bayaert, 1923.

Battandier, A., *Guide Canonique pour les Constitutions des Instituts à Voeux Simples*, 6. ed., Paris: Gabalda, 1923.

Bellarminus, Robertus, *Opera Omnia*, 8 vols., Neapoli: Pedone Lauriel, 1872.

Berutti, C., *Institutiones Iuris Canonici,* 6 vols., Vol. III, *De Religiosis,* Taurini-Romae: Marietti, 1936.

Beste, U., *Introductio in Codicem,* 3. ed., Collegeville, Minn.: St. John's Abbey Press, 1946.

Biederlack, J.—Führich, M., *De Religiosis,* Oeniponte: Rauch, 1919.

Bingham, Joseph, *The Antiquities of the Christian Church,* 2 vols., London, 1856.

Blat, A., *Commentarium Textus Codicis Iuris Canonici,* 5 vols. in 6, lib. II, pars II et III, *Ius de Religiosis,* 3. ed., Romae: apud "Angelicum," 1938.

Boak, Arthur, *A History of Rome to 565,* New York, 1923.

Bowe, Thomas, *Religious Superioresses,* The Catholic University of America Canon Law Studies, n. 228, Washington, D. C.: The Catholic University of America Press, 1946.

Brockhaus, Thomas, *Religious Who are Known as Conversi,* The Catholic University of American Canon Law Studies, n. 225, Washington, D. C.: The Catholic University of America Press, 1946.

Brown, J. V., *The Invalidating Effects of Force, Fear, and Fraud upon the Canonical Novitiate,* The Catholic University of America Canon Law Studies, n. 311, Washington, D. C.: The Catholic University of America Press, 1951.

Butler, Cuthbert, *Benedictine Monachism,* London: Longmans, Green and Co., 1919.

———, *Sancti Benedicti Regula Monasteriorum, Editio Critico- Practica,* Friburgi Brisgoviae, 1927.

Cappello, F. M., *Summa Iuris Canonici in Usum Scholarum Concinnata,* 3 vols., Romae: apud Aedes Universitatis Gregorianae, Vol. II, 4. ed., 1945.

Catholic Encyclopedia, The, 15 vols., Index and Supplement, New York, 1907-1922.

Cayré, F., *Manual of Patrology and History of Theology* (translated by H. Howitt), Tournai: Desclée and Co., 1931.

Cerato, P., *Censurae Vigentes Ipso Facto a Codice Iuris Canonici Excerptae,* 2. ed., Patavii: Typis Seminarii, 1921.

Chapman, John, *John Cassian,* Cambridge: Cambridge University Press, 1950.

———, *Saint Benedict and the Sixth Century,* London: Sheed and Ward, 1929.

Chelodi, Ioannes, *Ius Canonicum de Personis,* 3. ed. curavit Pius Ciprotti, Vicenza: Libreria Moderna Editrice, 1942.

Clancy, Patrick, *The Local Religious Superior,* The Catholic University of America Canon Law Studies, n. 175, Washington, D. C.: The Catholic University of America Press, 1943.

Clark, W. K., *The Lausiac History of Palladius,* London, 1918.

———, *Saint Basil the Great, A Study in Monasticism,* Cambridge, 1913.

Cocchi, G., *Commentarium in Codicem Iuris Canonici ad Usum Scholarum,* 5 vols. in 8, Liber II, Pars II, *De Religiosis,* 4. ed., Taurinorum Augustae: Marietti, 1946.

Coronata, Matthaeus Conte a, *Institutiones Iuris Canonici ad Usum Utriusque Cleri et Scholarum,* 4. ed., 5 vols., Vols. I et II, Taurini: Marietti, 1950-1951.

Creusen, J.—Garesche, E. F.—Ellis, A. C., *Religious Men and Women in the Code,* 4. ed., Milwaukee: Bruce, 1940.

Currier, C. W., History of Religious Orders, New York: Murphy and McCarthy, 1899.

De Meester, A., *Juris Canonici et Juris Canonico-Civilis Compendium,* 3 vols. in 4, Brugis: Desclée, 1921-1928, Vol. II, 1923.

Deroux, M. P., *Les Origines de l'Oblature bénédictine,* Les Editions de la Revue Mabillon, I, Viénne: Abbaye Saint-Martin de Ligugé, 1927.

Dubé, Arthur, *The General Principles for the Reckoning of Time in Canon Law,* The Catholic University of America Canon Law Studies, n. 144, Washington, D. C.: The Catholic University of America Press, 1941.

Fanfani, Ludovicus, *De Iure Religiosorum ad Normam Codicis Iuris Canonici,* 3. ed., Rovigo: Istituto Padano di Arti Grafiche, 1949.

Fernandez, J., *De Figura Juridica Ordinis Recollectorum S. Augustini,* Romae: apud Aedes Universitatis Gregorianae, 1938.

Ferreres, I., *Institutiones Canonicae iuxta Codicem Novissimum,* 2. ed., 2 vols., Barcinone, 1920.

Gill, Nicholas, *The Spiritual Prefect in Clerical Houses of Study,* The Catholic University of America Canon Law Studies, n. 216, Washington, D. C.: The Catholic University of America Press, 1945.

Goyeneche, S., *Iuris Canonici Summa Principia de Religiosis,* Romae: Tip. Pol. "Cuore di Maria," 1938.

Haring, J., *Grundzüge des katholischen Kirchenrechts,* 3. ed., 2 vols., Graz, 1924.

Heimbucher, Max, *Die Orden und Kongregationen der katholischen Kirche,* 3. ed., 2 vols., Paderborn: Schöningh, 1933-1934.

Hoffmann, Eberhard, *Das Konverseninstitut des Cisterzienserordens in seinem Ursprung und seiner Organisation,* Freiburger historische Studien, I, Freiburgi Br., 1905.

Jardi, A., *El Derecho de las Religiosas,* 2. ed., Vich: Editorial Serafico, 1927.

Kealy, Thomas, *The Dowry of Women Religious,* The Catholic University of America Canon Law Studies, n. 134, Washington, D. C.: The Catholic University of America Press, 1941.

Knowles, David, *The Monastic Order in England,* Cambridge: University Press, 1941.

Laudeuze, Palin, *Étude sur le Cénobitisme Pakhomien,* Louvain, 1898.

Leipoldt, Johannes, *Schenute von Atripe und die Entstehung des National-Aegyptischen Christentums,* Leipzig, 1903.

Leitner, M., *Handbuch des katholischen Kirchenrechts, Dritte Lieferung: Das Ordensrecht,* 2. ed., Regensburg: Kösel und Pustet, 1922.

Mackean, W. H., *Christian Monasticism in Egypt,* New York: Macmillan Co., 1920.

Malnory, Arthur, *St. Caesaire, Evêque d'Arles,* Paris, 1894.

Martène, Edmundus, *De Antiquis Ecclesiae Ritibus,* ed. novissima, 4 vols., Antuaerpiae-Venetiis, 1763-1764.

Martène, Edmundus—Durand, Ursinus, *Thesaurus Novus Anecdotorum,* 5 vols., Lutetiae Parisiorum, 1717.

McNeil, Thomas, *Religious of Diocesan Right* (unprinted Licentiate thesis), Washington, D. C.: The Catholic University of America, 1923-1924.

Montalambert, Charles, *The Monks of the West,* 8 vols., New York: Longmans, Green and Co., 1896.

Morison, B. D., *Saint Basil and His Rule,* London, 1912.

Mulhern, Philip, *The Early Dominican Lay Brother,* Washington, D. C.: (Dominican College), 1944.

Murphy, Sister Margaret Gertrude, *Saint Basil and Monasticism,* Washington, D. C.: The Catholic University of America, 1930.

Neale, J. M., *A History of the Eastern Church,* London, 1847.

Nicene and Post Nicene Fathers, Second Series, Vol. XI, New York: Christian Literature Co., 1894.

Nock, Sister Frances Clare, *Vita Sancti Fructuosi of St. Valerius, Abbot of San Pedro de Montes, with a Translation, Introduction and Commentary,* Studies in Mediaeval History, New Series, Vol. VII, Washington, D. C.: The Catholic University of America Press, 1946.

O'Brien, R., *The Provincial Superior in Religious Orders of Men,* The Catholic University of America Canon Law Studies, n. 258, Washington, D. C.: The Catholic University of America Press, 1947.

Oesterle, G., *Praelectiones Iuris Canonici,* I, Romae: apud Collegium S. Anselmi, 1931.

Pejška, J., *Ius Canonicum Religiosorum,* 3. ed., Friburgi Brisgoviae: Herder, 1927.

Piatus, Montensis, *Praelectiones Juris Regularis,* ed. Victorius ab Appeltern, 3. ed., 2 vols., Tornaci, 1906.

Pirhing, Ernricus, *Ius Canonicum in Quinque Libros Decretalium Distributum,* Dilingae, 1722.

Prümmer, D., *Manuale Iuris Canonici in Usum Scholarum,* 3. ed., Friburgi Brisgoviae: Herder, 1922.

Quiles, Ismael, *San Isidoro de Sevilla,* Buenos Aires-Mexico, Espasa-Calpe Argentina, S.A., 1945.

Raus, J. B., *Institutiones Canonicae iuxta Novem Codicem Iuris pro Scholis vel ad usum Privatum Synthetice Redactae,* 2. ed., Lugduni, Parisiis: Vitte, 1931.

Reiffenstuel, Anacletus, *Jus Canonicum Universum,* 5 vols. in 3, Venetiis, 1760.

Schaaf, V., *The Cloister,* The Catholic University of America Canon Law Studies, n. 13, Washington, D. C.: The Catholic University of America, 1921.

Schaefer, Timotheus, *Das Ordenrecht nach dem Codex Iuris Canonici,* Münster: Verlag der Aschendorffschen Verlagsbuchhandlung, 1923.

———, *De Religiosis ad Normam Codicis Iuris Canonici,* 4. ed., Romae: Typis Polyglottis Vaticanis, 1947.

Schmalzgrueber, Franciscus, *Ius Ecclesiasticum Universum,* 5 vols. in 12, Romae, 1843-1845.

Smith, I. G., *Christian Monasticism from the Fourth to the Ninth Century of the Christian Era,* London: Innes and Co., 1892.

Sole, *De Delictis et Poenis,* Rome-New York: Pustet, 1920.

Stanton, W. A., *De Societatibus sive Virorum sive Mulerium in Communi Viventium sine Votis,* 2. ed., Halifax: Major Seminary of the Sacred Heart of Mary, 1936.

Suarez, Franciscus, *Opera Omnia,* 28 vols., Paris: Vivès, 1856-1878.

Tabera, A., *Derecho de Los Religiosos,* Madrid: Editorial Colculsa, 1948.

Toso, A., *Ad Codicem Iuris Canonici Commentaria Minora,* 5 vols., Romae: Marietti, 1920-1927.

Vermeersch, A.—Creusen, J., *Epitome Iuris Canonici cum Commentariis ac Scholas et ad Usum Privatum,* 7. ed., 3 vols., Vol. I, Mechliniae-Romae: Dessain, 1949.

Vromant, G., *De Bonis Ecclesiae Temporalibus,* Louvain: Museum Lessianum, 1927.

Wernz, Franciscus X., *Ius Decretalium ad usum Praelectionum in Scholis Tertus Canonici sive Iuris Decretalium,* 6 vols. in 10, Romae-Prati, 1898-1914.

Wernz, F. X.-Vidal, P., *Ius Canonicum ad Codicis Normam Exactum,* 7 vols. in 8, Romae: apud Aedes Universitatis Gregorianae, Vol. III *De Religiosis,* 1933.

Articles

Anonymous, "Consultationes," *Apollinaris,* VII (1934), 492-499.

Anonymous, "Dying Postulants Cannot be Admitted to Profession," *AER,* C (1939), 447-452.

De Langogne, P., "De la profession religieuse anticipée *in articulo mortis,*" *Le Canoniste Contemporain,* XVIII (1895), 1-9.

Goyeneche, S., "De Transitu ad aliam Religionem," *CpR,* II (1921), 116-124, 140-148, 173-180.
———, "Annotationes," *CpR,* IV (1923), 260-265.
———, "Consultationes," *CpR,* I (1920), 51-52; V (1924), 154-166; VIII (1927), 31-35; XI (1930), 31-38; XIII (1932), 36-43; XIV (1933), 257-265, 351-358; *CpRM,* XIX (1938), 13-18; XX (1939), 18-21.
Hofmeister, P., "*Professio in articulo mortis* unter dem neuen Recht," *TPQ,* LXXIV (1921), 493-500.
Langonio, Pius, a, "De anticipata in articulo mortis professione religiosa," *Analecta Ecclesiastica,* II (1894), 498-499.
Larraona, A., "Commentarium Codicis," *CpR,* IV (1923), 9-14; VIII (1927), 164-176; XII (1931), 124-130; XV (1934), 359-367; *CpRM,* XVI (1935), 144-153, 223-227, 307-312, 377-381; XVII (1936), 9-19; XX (1939), 8-17, 72-83; XXI (1940), 145-152; XXIV (1943), 199-216; XXV (1944), 3-25.
———, "Consultationes," *CpR,* I (1920), 52-57, 179-181; III (1922), 8-16.
Maroto, P., "Annotationes," *CpR,* X (1929), 334-343.
Ott, Michael, "Schenute," *Catholic Encyclopedia,* XIII, 527.
Ramos, D., "De Conditione Saecularium in Domibus Religiosorum," *CpR,* VI (1925), 136-140, 187-190, 324-329.
Schweiger, P., "Quaestio Canonica," *CpR,* IV (1923), 140-145.
Shahan, Thomas J., "Caesarius of Arles," *Catholic Encyclopedia,* III, 135-137.
Steiger, Joseph, "De Propagatione et diffusione vitae religiosae synopsis historica," *Periodica,* XIII (1924), 29-60; 73-100; 153-180.
Vermeersch, A., "Religious Life," *Catholic Encyclopedia,* XII, 748-762.
———, "Quaestiones de Codice Canonico," *Periodica,* IX (1921), (1)-(34).
———, "De professione novitii vel probandi in articulo mortis," *Periodica,* XII (1923), (159-(162).
———, "Annotationes," *Periodica,* XXI (1932), 38-40.
Voltas, P., "De Aperienda, Directionis Causa, Superioribus Conscientia," *CpR,* I (1920), 83-92; 117-125, 145-151.
———, "Consultationes," *CpR,* II (1921), 220-225.

PERIODICALS

American Ecclesiastical Review, The (formerly *Ecclesiastical Review, The,* July, 1905—December, 1943), Philadelphia, 1889-1943; Washington, 1944—
Analecta Ecclesiastica, Romae, 1893-1911.
Apollinaris, Romae, 1928—
Commentarium pro Religiosis, Romae, 1920-1934; ab anno 1935, *Commentarium pro Religiosis et Missionariis.*

Le Canoniste Contemporain, Paris, 1878-1922.

Linzer-theologisch-praktische Quartalschrift, Linz, 1832—

Periodica de Religiosis et Missionariis, Brugis, 1905-1919; *Periodica de Re Canonica et Morali, utilia praesertim Religiosis et Missionariis*, Brugis, 1920-1927; *Periodica de Re Morali, Canonica, Liturgica*, Brugis, 1927-1936; Romae, 1937—

ALPHABETICAL INDEX

BIOGRAPHICAL NOTE

James Daniel McGuire was born on January 20, 1929, in Kansas City, Missouri. After finishing his elementary training at Our Lady of Good Counsel School in that city, he attended St. John's Preparatory Seminary, from which he graduated in 1946. He was then admitted to the Novitiate of the Order of Recollects of Saint Augustine, and made his religious profession on September 1, 1947. He completed his philosophical course in Saint Augustine's Monastery in Kansas City, Kansas, and his courses in theology in Tagaste Monastery in Suffern, New York, being ordained to the priesthood on May 29, 1954. He enrolled in the School of Canon Law at The Catholic University of America in September, 1954, and received the Baccalaureate Degree in Canon Law in June, 1955, and the Licentiate Degree in June, 1956.

CANON LAW STUDIES*

375. Kelleher, Rev. Francis T., A.B., J.C.L., Judicial expenses.
376. Bantigue, Rev. Pedro N., J.C.L., The Provincial Council of Manila of 1771. (Its text followed by a commentary on *Actio* II, *De Episcopis*)
377. Burns, Rev. Dennis J., J.C.L., Matrimonial indissolubility: contrary conditions.
378. Deutsch, Rev. Bernard F., J.C.L., Jurisdiction of pastors in the external forum.
379. Dunnivan, Rev. John P., A.B., J.C.L., Prejudicial attempts in pending litigation.
380. Ernst, Rev. Albert C., A.B., J.C.L., Free admission to church for sacred rites.
381. Frattin, Mr. Peter Louis, JC.L., The matrimonial impediment of impotence: occlusion of the spermatic ducts and vaginismus.
382. Henry, Rev. Charles W., O.S.B., A.B., S.T.L., J.C.L., Canonical relations between bishops and abbots at the beginning of the tenth century.
383. Hoffman, Rev. Lawrence J., A.B., S.T.B., J.C.L., Clergy conferences: Canon 131.
384. Markham, Rev. James, A.B., S.T.L., J.C.L., The Sacred Congregation of Seminaries and Universities of Studies.
385. McGrath, Rev. John J., A.B., LL.B., J.C.L., A comparative study of crime and its imputability in ecclesiastical criminal law and in American criminal law.
386. McGuire, Rev. James D., O.R.S.A., J.C.L., The postulancy.
387. Munday, Rev. James E., J.C.L., Ecclesiastical Property in Australia and New Zealand.
388. Murphy, Rev. Joseph P., A.B., J.C.L., The laws of the State of New York affecting church property.
389. Pickard, Rev. William M., J.C.L., Judicial experts: a source of evidence in ecclesiastical trials.
390. Ruddy, Rev. James, J.C.L., The Apostolic Constitution *Christus Dominus*: text, translation and commentary, with short annotations on the Motu Proprio *Sacram Communionem*.
391. Vanyo, Rev. Leo V., A.B., J.C.L., Requisites of intention in the reception of the sacraments.

* For a complete list of the available numbers of this series apply to the Catholic University of America Press, 620 Michigan Avenue, N.E., Washington (17), D.C., for a general catalogue.

www.ingramcontent.com/pod-product-compliance
Lightning Source LLC
LaVergne TN
LVHW050233080826
844660LV00012B/523

* 9 7 8 0 8 1 3 2 2 5 4 6 3 *